MY SO

BLOOMERS

CW00519839

Charleston, SC
www.PalmettoPublishing.com

My Socks and Bloomers
Copyright © 2022 by Richard T. Henry

All rights reserved

No portion of this book may be reproduced, stored in
a retrieval system, or transmitted in any form by any
means–electronic, mechanical, photocopy, record-
ing, or other–except for brief quotations in printed
reviews, without prior permission of the author.

First Edition

Hardcover ISBN: 979-8-8229-0546-7
PaperbackISBN: 979-8-8229-0547-4
ebook ISBN: 979-8-8229-0548-1

MY SOCKS & BLOOMERS

RICHARD T. HENRY

I would like to dedicate this book to my great-grandmother, Julia Jones, and all twelve of her children.

-Richard T. Henry

INTRODUCTION

How does it really feel to be labeled something that you are not? I have made excuses all my life…. Stop! Before we go any further, let me introduce myself. I am Richard Terrell Henry aka Diddard. I was born in January of 1979, in Little Rock, Arkansas. It was one Tuesday morning when I made my entrance into this world. My mom went from being a happy mom to a frightened, scared new mom in minutes. See, I was born with meningococcal meningitis, and they did not expect me to make it. However, I miraculously survived, and my mother Denise was very grateful. The name that I knew and went by most of my adult life was Terrell, because I did not want to know Richard. I was a sad little boy who was just lost, but I will explain that more later. I was raised mostly by my grandmother who I called, "Mama." I always wanted to be a male version of her, so I always found myself dressed in her shoes and clothes. I even sometimes tried on her wigs. She would always take me to work with her, and she always kept me dressed nicely with a bowtie. Her coworkers loved that I wore a bowtie all the time. My grandmother always wore heels and suits which normally consisted of a blazer, blouse, and skirt. I remember when she worked at the bank on Broadway in Little Rock; baby she would tip through there in her heels and all eyes would be on her and me! It was like we owned the room. She would smile, nod her head, and tip on. I would walk closely behind her, imitating her.

My grandmother once worked at IHOP with a great deal of our family members, but one of her sisters, Aunt Fanny, really ran the store. She had great customer service, knew the customers, and knew the menu inside and out. Aunt Fanny provided me with my first example of great customer service at its finest. My granny had eight sisters, and I found myself always with one of them. Even when I would be with my uncles, Smoove and Dee, I would gravitate to their girlfriends. For some strange reason during this time in my life, I felt more comfortable being around females. I always felt different, weird, and ugly which caused me to always have my lips poked out. I would ask myself, *"Why can't I be more like Mama and Aunt Fanny, and have a smile on my face full of happiness?"*

Now here is where a normal person would probably tell you about his elementary school years, but I cannot seem to remember anything about it. It's like there is a total block in my memory. However, I can remember my junior high school years quite well. During junior high, I was not very popular, but my sister was. My younger sister and her friends were like the "mean girls"of the school. Most people knew me as her older "gay" brother. It was odd to be described as gay because I did not even know that I was gay yet. I knew I was different, but I did not think I was gay. This time was difficult, because it was like I did not even have an identity without my sister, and that identity was flawed because I was not even gay, or was I?

My only refuge away from the drama of school and home (which I will get into more later) was with my Aunt RiRi, my mom's half-sister. This was an exciting time for me. Aunt RiRi lived in Wrightsville, Arkansas. This is the more rural part of the state. In Wrightsville, I enjoyed visiting all her different family members' houses. I can still remember tasting the chitterlings, with mustard and hot sauce. I would eat so much of those chitterlings until Aunt RiRi's mom would say, "Don't bring Terrell down here eatin' up my pot of chittlins." These were indeed some of the best times for me. My Aunt RiRi also loved going to church. I remember going to First Baptist Church, which sat at the end of the street where her family lived. We would go every Sunday that I was with her, and when we returned from church, Aunt RiRi's mom would have dinner already finished and waiting for us. Aunt RiRi was also a teacher at my junior high school, Mabelvale Junior High. She would pick me up in the mornings for school and bring me home from school because I was insecure and did not want to ride the bus. On the bus, I would be teased and called, "fag". I would find any excuse to avoid that trauma, and lucky for me, Aunt RiRi did not mind picking me up. After some time, she noticed how I would begin to get sad whenever she would take me home from school or her house. One day when I was about to get out of the car, she touched my lap and said, "What's wrong? I have noticed that whenever I bring you home, you become instantly sad." I replied, "Nothing." My aunt quickly snapped back with, "Don't you lie to me! As long as he does not touch my sister, everything will be okay." I remember sitting there thinking, "How does she know that something is wrong?" These rides and visits with Aunt RiRi continued until she had her third child, which happened to be a boy. After my little cousin was born, things went back to normal for me, and the awkwardness and feeling like I did not belong returned. It continued so much until I found myself living with my great Aunt TC.

Aunt TC lived in Cleveland, Ohio. She was a school teacher with a great personality who happened to have a daughter. Her daughter Sheesh was not enthused by my presence at all. She felt like I was taking advantage of her mom and taking away from her. Hence, I had a very short stay in Cleveland that time. I had three other great aunts that lived in Cleveland too. I spent a great deal of time with them and their families. I loved my aunts dearly, but some of the family members made me feel unwelcomed, and some of them even called me a "punk". This constant name calling caused me to feel even more out of place and unwanted. While my constant travels as a child made me feel this way, I later learned that everyone wanted me around. They actually began asking for me to visit.

Not only was my Aunt TC in Cleveland, but my Aunt Bubbles was there too. I really loved and adored this aunt because she was the BEST cook in the family. Unfortunately, she was never in a good mood. This aunt was always fussing and cussing because either someone had taken something out of her purse, they had stolen her car, or they had taken her medicine bottles. You could often hear her screaming, "Stay out of my purse and leave my damn painkillers alone!!!" I felt bad for her, and I wished that things were better for her! Seeing her upset caused me to really regret the times that I had gone into my grandmother's purse and stolen her car keys.

There was one more aunt that I loved being around! That was my great aunt Janice. Aunt Janice lived in this lavishly decorated house, that through my kid eyes appeared to be a mansion. This mansion had a four-car garage that housed several expensive cars. I remember taking great pleasure in washing their cars. I would wash the cars and then line them up in their curved driveway according to how I thought they were valued. Her husband, Roy, reminded me of Uncle Phil from the *Fresh Prince of Bel-Air*. Uncle Roy was a clean-cut man, and he was always dressed in khakis and a buttoned up shirt with some nice shoes. Sometimes, he also wore a bowtie when he would leave the house. Come to think of it, I never remember seeing him wear jeans. Uncle Roy and Aunt Janice had three sons. I really admired their oldest son, Roy Jr. Roy Jr. was an athlete, a lady's man, and he also allowed me to ride around with him. He was one of the few males in my family that I admired. I really wanted to be more like him, but he was more masculine than me. Being around all these masculine men made me feel weird and made me question even more where I belonged. I would always try to follow Roy Jr., because I hoped that his influence would possibly magically make me become more masculine. Even though I desired to be around him, I still found myself around my aunt and her friends more. I would always hear Uncle Phil (Uncle Roy) say, "Don't take him with you. You should leave him here with the boys." She never did though. I had great times in Cleveland, but it just did not work out.

After my stay in Cleveland ended, I found myself back in Little Rock. Now, I am a fifteen-year-old searching for my identity, and I am living with my mom and her husband. My stepdad always had his lips poked out. I remember telling him one time, "You better stick your lip in, or I will step on it." I was hoping that would cause him to smile, but it didn't. My stepdad and I were not able to find common ground. After a few short weeks, I was sent to my grandmother's house. Shortly after I returned to live with my grandmother, I began to have some vivid nightmares. I began to realize that these nightmares were flashbacks from my early childhood. In the nightmares, I would be at my cousin Tiwan's house, on Battery Street. I remember I loved being around my aunt (his mom) because she always made me feel welcomed. In the nightmares, I was my cousin Tiwan's personal punching bag (I guess that was foreshadowing because he is a professional boxer today). When I was not being his punching bag, his friends were touching and grabbing on me whenever he was not around. In one of the dreams, I was five years old, and I remembered someone pulling me under a bed. Once under the bed, he began to hunch me. I only shared the details from these nightmares with my cousin, Vinny. Vinny was my great uncle's daughter. I spent a lot of time with my great uncle, Bubba, and his family. These nightmares began to awaken something within me which caused me to question my sexuality and my desire to explore.

CHAPTER ONE

It was one chilly morning! I remember waking up thinking about watching the Young and the Restless. As I laid there waiting on the show to come on, my uncle came waltzing his ass through the door. He began to fuss at me. He asked, "What are you doing here? Why aren't you at home?" I replied, "Mama said I could stay here." My uncle quickly snapped back with, "That's not your Mama. She's your grandmama! Where is she anyway?" I quickly said, "That's your mama, you should know." My uncle turned and walked out the door. After he was gone, I lost all desires to watch my soaps. I decided to call my Aunt Fanny. On the other end of the phone, my aunt began to sing, "Terrrelll!!! What's the tea Greta?" To which I replied, "Nothing much! I was trying to watch the *Young and the Restless*, but my uncle came in questioning why I was in his mama's bed and not at home." Then, I asked my aunt, "Do you think there's something wrong with me being at my grandma's and not at home?" My aunt chirped back, "Why aren't you at your mom's?" I told my aunt that I didn't know exactly why, but I knew that I didn't feel comfortable at my mom's. My aunt began to laugh hysterically. My aunt said, "Chile, I remember the other day when your uncle walked up to your grandma. He called himself whispering, but I heard him clear as day. He said, 'Mama, I believe Diddard is a queer.'" Out of nowhere, I heard my aunt's dog, Fefe, barking loudly. Aunt Fanny told me, "Baby I got to go. There must be someone at my door." As soon as I hung up with my aunt, I heard a knock at my grandma's door.

I jumped up and ran to the door. When I opened it, there were my three little male cousins standing there. As I looked out the door, all I could see was a car peeling off! I closed the door, and I called my grandma at work. I explained to her what happened. As I was explaining the circumstances, I quickly began to realize that my stay was ending, but I didn't know just yet how close the end was near. After our phone call ended, I went to the front room, and I laid down on the sofa. While laying on the sofa, I began realizing that my sixteenth birthday was quickly approaching. As I considered my birthday, I began to remember my fifteenth -birthday party, and I suddenly began to feel my stomach doing somersaults. These somersaults were summoned by the emotions that I remembered feeling at my last party. We had posted flyers all over the school inviting people to my birthday party. The flyers were only up for a few hours. I initially thought that they were taken down by the "straights" who always called me "Fag." However, I later learned that the school administration removed the flyers. The day of my party arrives, and I am so excited to celebrate. This excitement was very short-lived, because only four people came. I vividly recall how many people were there, because ALL four of them were sandwiched in my grandma's car as we drove to her house for my party. These same four individuals used me for rides, because I was the only black kid with a car. I wanted friends so badly that I would ride them around with me all the time. I would even have them in the car with me when I would pick my grandma up for work. She would be so pissed at me every time I would roll up to pick her up from work. Mama would always say, "Got Damn it! Didn't I tell you not to have all these niggas in my car!" She would just sit in the car with her lips poked out the whole ride home!

That evening my uncle began to fuss at me saying, "You keep giving my mama heartache and pain!" My grandmama decided to send me on an errand to give him time to calm down. She sent me to her baby brother's house to get a plate of his wife's home cooked dinner. However, as my other uncle would say, "I turned a few extra corners." I ended up at my cousin Cuna's house. We got in the car and started riding around. As we were riding, the music began to play on the radio, and Dottie Peoples began to sing, "He's an On Time God!" My cousin quickly took the cassette tape out, and she put in Al B Sure's, "Off on Your Own Girl." She hated riding with me listening to gospel music, but gospel music always made me feel safe. Therefore, I always listened to it when I was driving my grandma's car. Finally, we made it to my uncle's house. When we walked in, we were welcomed by the aroma of the food. I still remember smelling her buttermilk pie. She had buttermilk pies, carrot cakes, and several other desserts on a table by her kitchen. Vinny came and hugged both of us. While we were chatting it up with her, the phone began to ring. My heart instantly dropped because I knew it was my grandma calling about her car. Surprisingly, she was more worried about the food. On that note, I decided to drop some food off to her. When I pulled up at my grandma's house, my youngest uncle was sitting on the steps waiting. When he realized that Cuna was in the car with me, he said, "See, you need to take your ass home to your mama!"

By the time I made it back to the house, my uncles were gone, and my grandma was stuffed and laying in her bed. I crawled into bed with her. As soon as I began to get comfortable, the phone started ringing. It was one of her sisters. They began to gossip, and I just sat there listening attentively. While talking to her sister, she jokingly told me, "Go down there and suck my toe while you are sitting here listening to my conversation." I could hear her sister on the phone laughing. Her sister said, "You must be talking to Diddard." By this time, one of my uncles walked into the room. As he was walking in, my grandma let out one of the loudest farts I ever heard. My uncle said, "Ugh! Diddard, how are you laying there while mama farting?" I told him, "It doesn't stink, it smells like flowers." My uncle snapped back, "No, it doesn't! It smells like rotten eggs!" Then he asked, "Mama can I hold ten dollars and borrow your car? I need to turn a couple of corners." While fussing at him for asking to borrow the money and her car, she was digging into her purse looking for the money and her car keys. While my uncle was leaving the room, my grandma had a beep on the phone. It was her other sister calling. She clicked over and told that sister that they would call her back on three-way. Once all three of them were on the phone, I began to get anxious because I knew there was going to be some juicy gossip. As I sat there drooling, anticipating each word, I heard a small squeaky voice from outside yelling, "Ames! Ames!" It was my great grandmother. She was outside calling my grandmama because she couldn't get her on the phone. My great-grandmother wanted some wings from KFC, but my uncle was already gone in the car. My grandmama ended the call with her sisters, and she went across the street to check on her mom and let her know that my uncle was gone in the car. I saw this as a great opportunity to play dress up. I quickly darted into her closet and grabbed one of her dresses and a pair of her nice high heels. I slipped the dress on quickly, and as I was beginning to slip on the left high heel, I heard the door closed. Luckily, she went into the kitchen first. In a rush to take off the dress, I ripped it because I couldn't unzip the zipper. I took the dress, balled it up, and threw it in the very back of the closet. My nerves began to get the best of me, so I tipped across the street to my great grandmother's house. I walked into her house, and I went into her bedroom and sat on the bed. My great-grandmother came out of her bathroom, and she began to yell, "Get off my bed! That isn't for sitting! It is for laying down! Then, you have your jeans on!" My great-grandmother couldn't finish fussing at me because her phone started ringing. She answered it and it was one of her daughters complaining about one of her sister's behavior. Then, I heard a car pulling up. I looked out the window, and it was my uncle coming back with the car. I went back to my grandmama's house, and I asked if I could go get the wings for her mom. She told me, "Yes, but you better come straight back here!"

In a pinch, I was cruising down the road in my grandma's 1993 emerald green Toyota Camry. Tonight was different from many other nights because tonight, I wasn't blasting my normal gospel music, and I was riding solo for once. I also had the radio turned down low with the windows down. As I was enjoying the wind blowing, I suddenly heard some music off in the distance. All I could hear was, "Ooo la-la-la, it's the way that you feel when you know that it's real." These lyrics danced through the radio from Teena Marie's voice, and they lured my eyes to this house that I had always avoided making eye contact with. I can still hear my uncle's girlfriend telling me, "That's a house where the queers hangout!" Those words caused my teenage eyes to fear glancing if only for a moment at this house. However, tonight was very different, because Teena Marie was calling me, and I had to take at least one glance.

This one glance would be the beginning of a lifetime of experiences. As I looked at the forbidden house, I began to see figures swaying to the music. I remember thinking, "Are my eyes playing tricks on me?" With a closer look, I realized that the figures were men dressed in towels as headwraps, bedspreads, and dresses, and some of them were dressed in women's clothing. I didn't know what to do. I was so engrossed with watching them sway and dance to Teena Marie that I took my eyes completely away from the road until I felt a sudden jolt of the car. This jolt was caused by me hitting the curve. I panicked! I quickly pulled into the KFC parking lot to check the car. Luckily, everything was fine. Just as I was about to pick my head up from checking the tire, I heard a very deep voice say, "Are you okay?" I turned around and there was this beautiful Puerto Rican man walking up to me. As my eyes began to adjust to the beauty that stood before me, I could feel my member downstairs begin to slowly grow with each step he made towards me. After examining this man more closely, I noticed that he was a tall man with curly hair, smooth shea butter skin, a flawless chiseled body, and all of this was adorned with a sneaky smirk. His body movements were distinctively feminine which didn't match his voice. I felt like I was looking at a piece of art, trying to understand it. Once I was able to gather myself, I quickly told him, "I am fine." He replied by saying, "I am Leon." After I told him my name, he wrote his number down on a receipt, and he skated into KFC.

As I began to walk into the KFC, our eyes locked again, and he followed my every step. He continued to watch me with that sneaky smirk. He got his food and walked out. After he was gone, the cashier asked her coworkers, "Did y'all see that fag?" These words made me tremble with fear. In my head I asked myself, "*Did they see us talking outside, do they know that I am struggling with my sexuality too, and will they talk about me when I leave?*" Once I got in my car, my mind went straight to Leon. I couldn't wait to get home and call him. I was praying that my grandma wasn't on the phone.

After dropping the food off to my great-grandmother, I quickly ran into my grandmama's house, only to find her on the phone with two of her sisters. This time they were gossiping about one of the oldest sisters. I overheard my grandmama say, "Child she's about to have another surgery." After hearing that I thought to myself, "*Po thang*!" As I began to walk away, I could hear, "Wheeeeeeel ooof Fortune" coming from the living room tv. My grandmama must have heard it too because she told her sisters, "Let me get off this phone. I didn't realize that it was getting this late in the evening. I have to get over to Mrs. D so she can do this here hair of mine." I couldn't wait for her to leave so I could get to the phone to call Leon. My grandmama suspected something was going on, because I would normally insist that I ride with her. However, I was content with staying behind. Mama looked me and said, "Wait a minute!" I could see the wheels turning in her head. I went about my business as normal. As soon as I heard the car pull off, I raced to grab the phone! As I threw myself on her bed and reached for it, my hand landed on the table. I looked over and the phone was gone! Mama must have hid it from me because I was known to make long distance phone calls on her phone or any other phone that I could get my hand on. I just rolled over and poked my lips out.

After laying there for a few minutes, I came up with a great idea. I jumped up and began to ramble around the house for some coins. I could go call him on one of the payphones. Once I found some coins, I quickly ran up the street to the nearest payphone. The closer I got to the payphone; my smile began to turn upside down again. There was a long line waiting on the payphone. I remember thinking, "*Just my damn luck*!" I stood there patiently waiting and finally it was my turn. I dropped the quarter in the payphone, and I waited anxiously. Then, I heard, "Beep Beep Beep!" It was busy! I dropped another quarter and tried again. This time, it began to ring. Next thing I know, I heard a lady's voice saying, "Hello! Who are you?" I said, "Terrell." The voice then said, "How do you know my son? It doesn't matter anyway. I am on the phone." Then, I heard the phone click as she hung up. I was over it! I decided to walk to my uncle's house because I wanted to see if his girlfriend was cooking.

As I approached my uncle's house, I saw his girlfriend's daughter, Asia, and her boyfriend, Juan. They were sitting on the porch. He was a light skinned pretty boy with a distinctive mole on his face, and he had a high top with a low side. It reminded me of the dude from the movie Juice. As soon as I made it to their porch, a black Camaro pulled up to the house with a bald head guy that reminded you of someone's poster boy Sugar Daddy. To my surprise, Juan jumped into the car, and they drove off. I looked at Asia and asked her, "Who was that Sugar Daddy?" Asia told me, "His name is Prince." Before I could ask her any additional questions, her dad pulled up, she jumped in the car, and with a flash they were gone. I remember standing there thinking, "*I wish my dad would come pick me up.*" But I quickly remembered that I didn't know who my father was yet, and I was always told that his wife didn't want to have anything to do with me. Therefore, he chose to stay away too. After Asia left, I tried to hang out with my uncle and Asa's mom, but my uncle was fast asleep, and his girlfriend was bored. I decided to walk home.

As I was walking down the street, a black Pontiac Sunfire slowly crept beside me. As Tweet would say, "I looked over to my left." When I looked to my left, it was a car full of gay boys. It kind of reminded me of the cars I had seen before packed with clowns popping out of it. One of the boys yelled out of the car, "Hey boy! Let me suck that bird!" I stood there confused as hell, as the car sped off. As the car drove away, I remember thinking, "*That car looks so familiar! Where do I know it from?*" I can also still remember thinking, "*What in the hell is a bird? How are you going to suck it?*" After a few minutes of confusion, I decided to continue walking to my grandmama's house.

I made it to my grandmama's house, and I decided to try to reach Leon again, but he didn't answer. I laid across the bed and I was thinking, "*I can't take this! I have to try to reach him again.*" I am not sure why, but I had this pressing urge to talk to him. And I felt an unfamiliar tingly that ran up from my groin area that traveled vigorously up my spine. Unfortunately, my uncle was on the phone. I decided to run across the street to my great grandmother's house, but as I reached for the front doorknob, I heard my younger cousins arguing. I went to see what they were doing, and they were in the kitchen fighting over some oatmeal packets. My grandmama loved feeding us oatmeal. She fed us so much of it until I hated the smell of it. Their dad walked in, and they both immediately got quiet. He walked in the room and looked at me. He asked, "What are you doing?" I replied, "Minding my business. What are you doing?" He knew that I was looking for the phone because he was too. Then, my grandmama walked into the room with the phone in her hand. My uncle asked her, "Mom, can I borrow the car?" I followed with, "May I use the phone?" As soon as she plugged the phone in the wall, it began to ring. It was her sister, Aunt Fanny. She called to talk business about her restaurant. I walked outside and sat on the porch. While sitting there thinking about Leon and wishing I could hear his voice, the same black car from earlier drove by. They blew the horn as they drove by. Then, it dawned on me, "*Those are the queers that live on 12th street that my uncle's girlfriend always warned me about.*" I started to walk their way, and I saw that older dude, Prince and Asia's boyfriend, Juan. Something didn't seem right, and I felt a little jealousy begin to rise because I was wondering why Juan was riding with Prince. As I got closer to the forbidden house, I heard loud music booming. I remember it sounded like Lisa Fischer. Then, I heard a horn blowing. It was my cousin, Vinny. She was in a brand-new red Pontiac Sunfire. My great-grandmother helped her get the car. I couldn't understand why she helped her get a new car, but she did. I jumped in the car, and we began to hit a couple of corners. Then, we ended up at her house. They had a dial up computer, so I logged on AOL. I had an AOL chat buddy that lived in Jackson, Tennessee. I enjoyed chatting with him from time to time. If only I had a car, I would have visited him. However, we just mailed letters and pictures to each other. Suddenly, I heard a car pull up. It was my granny coming to pick up her baby brother. Once I learned that they were going to the soul food restaurant, Frankie's, I quickly logged off and joined them in the car. I never pass up on a good meal!

After finishing a fabulous meal, my mind quickly returned to Leon. As soon as I got back to the phone, I called him. His sister answered the phone, and she quickly asked, "Are you gay?" I hung up the phone, and I sat there for a moment to think about my actions. I began to question, "*Am I gay*?" I felt like my mind was racing. I began to feel like I didn't know who I was or where I belonged. I called my mom. When I called, my little brother answered the phone. Hearing his voice made my spirits come up, and I wanted to go home. However, I quickly remembered my stepdad, and I wondered how he would respond to my homecoming. Then, I heard my stepdad's daughter in the background asking to use the phone. This sparked my anger, and I hung the phone up without saying anything. I felt tears forming in my eyes, but my little cousin, Little D, walked up to me. He always made me smile because I was always thinking that he was flipping me off. Little D's finger was broken, and no one had ever taken him to get it checked. Therefore, every time he scratched his face, it looked like he was sticking up his middle finger. It made me smile every time. He hugged me which comforted me. I climbed into bed on a full stomach and quickly fell fast asleep.

The next morning, I woke up early. It was Sunday morning, and I was excited to go to church with my great grandmother. Most of the family seemed to avoid going to church with her, but my great grandmother, Vinny, Aunt Fanny, and I always enjoyed going to church. After getting dressed, I went across the street to my great grandmother's house. I walked into the house to the aroma of breakfast cooking, but she hadn't cooked anything I wanted to eat, so I decided to go into the living room to use her phone. I tried to call Leon again, but the line was busy again. I almost decided to just give up, but I decided to give it one more try. This time, the phone rang, and a guy answered. The voice on the other end of the phone made me tingle. I instantly knew it was him. As soon as I said, "Hello! May I speak to Leon?" My great-grandmother picked up the phone in another room screaming, "Get off my phone! Don't be on my phone making long distance calls!" I was done! It seemed like everyone was trying to keep me away from him. I quickly hung up the phone and walked into the den where she was. I assured my great grandmother that I wasn't making any long-distance calls. She asked me, "Who is Leon?" and I didn't know how to answer that because I didn't know who he was yet. As we approached the church, my great granny popped a piece of butterscotch in her mouth and began to tell a funny story. We all laughed as we got out of the car. That's when I saw my mom and stepdad pull up in their Cadillac. My mouth dropped! They don't ever come to church. When we walked in, I was shocked again because my grandmother and her best friend were sitting in the back. My grandmother was sitting there in her fur smacking on gum, while her best friend, Ms. Shell was sitting there cutting out coupons. I asked her, "Why are you cutting coupons in church?" She humorously replied, "To stay woke and ignore your granny smacking on her gum." I asked my granny, "Why are all y'all here today?" She informed me that my mom and stepdad were joining church today. I was wondering if that would change anything with my mom and stepdad. When church was over, I started noticing that there were quite a few gay people at church. I had never noticed this before, but today I did. I am not even sure how I knew this, but they kept looking at me. The more I looked at them, the more I wanted to call and talk to Leon. We ended up back at Vinny's house for dinner. Once dinner was done, I ended up going home with my mom. We stopped at the store, and I saw a guy from school that everyone always teased. It wasn't as bad for me, because unlike him, I didn't walk like a girl. Because they called him a fag, I made sure to keep my distance. He called my name, but I kept walking trying to avoid him. I didn't answer because I didn't want my mom to ask me about him, but she kept walking. Finally, I had no other choice but to speak to him, because he walked right up to me. He said, "Hey Terrell! I thought that was you. I am not sure if you know my name, but I am Ant." We talked for a few and exchanged numbers. As soon as I made it to my mom's, the phone began to ring. I answered the phone, and it was Ant. When I heard his voice over the phone, my body cringed! I wanted to hear a masculine voice, and he was soft and it sounded like he was a woman. However, I decided to chat with him for a few minutes. After a few minutes of conversation, he asked to hang out. I agreed to hang out. Thirty minutes later, he pulled up in his mom's car, and we were off to Kanis Park. Kanis Park was notorious for guys hooking up. It was like Atlanta's Piedmont Park at nightfall.

He found a nice, secluded area to park. Once he parked, his hands began to slowly rub up my left thigh. I sat there without any response. My member just laid there like a dog in the sun on a hot, sunny day. I remember thinking, "Why is he touching me? I am only looking for a friend." I finally got the nerve up to stop him from touching me. When I reached over to stop his hand, he said, "Oh my bad!" I replied, "Is this what all gay dudes do? Do you just rub on each other?" Ant looked at me with a confused look and said, "I'm sorry! I thought you were attracted to me too." I instantly replied with, "I thought you only wanted to hang out. I was looking for a friend." Ant smiled and said, "Well, I guess I have a new big sister then." I quickly corrected him by saying, "No! I can be your big brother."

Once we got an understanding that this was a platonic friendship, I began to tell him about my feelings for Leon. Ant began to laugh, and said, "That's a whore that's been spreading diseases all around the city. Chile, that dude has slept with folks' men and everything." Once I heard his disapproval of Leon, I quickly changed the subject. Since I was new to the scene, I asked him about his love life and his past lovers. He told me about all his boyfriends, his sexual encounters, and the undercover guys that were at school. After a few more minutes of him filling me in with the latest gossip, he turned the car on, and we drove out of the park.

As we drove, he continued teaching me about the lifestyle. I was so engrossed in the conversation that I didn't pay any attention to where we were going. When I looked up, I gagged! We were sitting in the driveway of the house that I have always tried to avoid looking at... *the house where the queers lived.*

CHAPTER TWO

Ant turned the car off and jumped out. After a few seconds, he looked back and saw me still sitting there. He turned around and said, "Chile get out of that car! There's nothing here to be scared of." I slowly opened the door and stepped out of the car. Now that I think about it, it was like I was moving in slow motion. I remember feeling the ground thinking that it felt different. It felt unfamiliar, and I could feel my knees shaking. We walked down a path, and he just opened the door. As we walked in, I began to scan the room with my eyes. There were eight of them sitting in the living room. When we walked in, I could feel them just looking at me. All their eyes were on me. I felt like I was the only living person in a zombie movie. As I continued to scan the room, I noticed that most of the guys were very feminine. There was only one masculine man there. He was sitting there staring at a beer can in his hand and shaking his leg. It seemed like he too was nervous. I tried not to look at him. Out of nowhere, I heard someone say, "Who is this new cute face that you have brought over here, Ant?" Then, she or he, looked at me and asked me, "How old are you?" I didn't know then if it was a woman or man. He looked like a girl, but his body said something different. This person was tall, muscular, with a deep voice. However, he or she had on a wig, makeup, and very long nails.

As I took a deep breath to answer the question, I felt a gust of wind pass me. I looked to my right, and the straight acting man wasn't sitting there in the chair anymore, and the card table chair was laying on the floor. As the door slammed, one of the guys leaped up and ran to the back of the house yelling someone's name. Within seconds, another manly guy with a wig on stormed out saying, "Damn! I can't even pee!" As he dashed out the door, everyone else in the house began to run to the window except me. I was so scared, so I decided to sit on one of the card table chairs. I was so ready to leave. Everyone began to get louder and louder. One of them said, "I told that bitch stop bringing trade over here!"

Then, we heard a loud scream. Everyone started screaming, "They are fighting!" The next thing I know, everyone was running out the door. I looked out the window, and I saw the guy with a wig laying on the ground. I jumped up and ran out the front door. As I was walking home, I began to feel something wet on my leg. That's when I realized that I must have been so scared that I peed on myself. As I was walking home, I heard a horn blow. I was so shaken that I kept walking. Then, I heard my name. I looked up and it was Leon with another guy riding shotgun. My heart dropped, but it stopped midway, because I was trying to see who was sitting where I should be sitting. I climbed into the back seat, and he drove off. As we drove, I was conflicted. I couldn't shake what I had just witnessed, and I wanted to know who was riding with Leon. I sat in the backseat with my head down. Leon asked me, "What's wrong?" I didn't know how to answer that question. I didn't know which bothered me more, what I had witnessed or the asshole in my man's car. That's when Leon turned and looked at me. He then said, "Oh! I forgot! This is my godsister, Day Day!"

His sister? I was confused! I just shook my head. As Day Day began to speak, we were pulling up to a house. It was Day Day's house. They stopped there because he wanted to check his messages, check the caller ID, and to see if his mom was cooking dinner which happened to be right up my alley. Once we parked, we sat for a minute, because Leon wanted to know what was bothering me. Day Day was reaching for the door handle, but once he heard Leon ask me, "What's wrong?" for the second time, he stopped and decided to listen to my answer. Before I could tell them, I instantly felt a warmth in my crotch area. In all of the excitement, I had completely forgotten that I had peed on myself when I saw the guy's near lifeless body laying on the grass. I didn't know what to do next, because I needed to go home and change, but I didn't want to let him know that I had peed on myself.

Luckily, I was saved by a knock on the window. It was Day Day's mom. She slid some money through the window to Day Day, and she said, "Baby go to the store and get me some eggs." As we drove down the street for the eggs, I finally found the nerve to share with them what I had just witnessed. While the words slid slowly off my nervous lips, they both began to laugh with excitement. Then, they began to yell, "Bitch!!!" I couldn't believe their reactions to the horror that I had just witnessed. I poked my lip out and I asked Leon, " Will you please take me home?" That's when they said, "Wait a minute, we want to hear the rest of this story." I said, "Please just take me home." They looked at each other, apologized and said, "We have to break you into the "life". You are a little fragile and timid. You have to have some tough skin and a mouth to survive around these girls." In my mind, I remember thinking to myself, " This is not the life that I want to live."

We made it to the grocery store, and Day Day ran in to grab the eggs. While he was gone, Leon and I sat in the car in total silence. A few minutes later, Day Day returned with the eggs, and we pulled out of the parking lot. We drove about a block or so before Leon pulled up to a payphone. He got out of the car and made a quick call. When he returned to the car, he looked at Day Day and said, " Bitch I need to make this coin. Drop me off at Prince's house and come back to get me." I was surprised! He was going to just leave me like this. Once we pulled up to the house, I was shocked because it was the guy that picked up my cousin's boyfriend a few days prior. I thought I would be jealous, but I wasn't. This was only a wake up call for me, because it let me know that it wasn't anything. After the last few days, if this is what "life" or the gay life is about, I don't want any parts of it. Once Leon got out of the car, Day Day slid over to the driver seat, and I jumped in the passenger seat. Day Day decided to put a tape in the cassette player. It happened to be a gospel song. He said, "This always puts me in a good mood." The next thing I know I could hear this woman say, "In God there is no failure......." Turns out the song changed my mood too. The next thing I know, I was tapping my foot and singing along with the song. I looked over and Day Day was rocking and singing like he was the original singer of the song. As we rode down Broadway clapping our hands and singing, we heard a siren in the background of the music. We both turned around to see some blue lights following us. We were only a few blocks away from Day Day's house. As the cop approached the window, a second car pulled up. The first cop began to question Day Day. He asked, "May I have your license?" Unfortunately, he didn't have his license. He gave the police officer his social security number. While the officer was gone to check his social, Day Day told me that he needed to get in contact with his mom. I reached in my pockets, but I realized that I didn't have any change. By this time, the officer returned to the car. He told Day Day to get out of the car. The next thing I know, he was putting him in handcuffs. The second officer came over to my window, and he apologized to me. He said, "I am so sorry that you have been put in this situation. The car registration is expired, there isn't any insurance on file, and the driver has a warrant out for his arrest. We are going to have to impound this car." I could feel the tears falling on my face, because I didn't know what to do. What else could happen in this one day?

I got out of the car and began to walk towards Day Day's house to let his mom know what happened. When I reached the house, I knocked on the door. When she opened the door,

I was so scared and nervous that she couldn't understand what I was saying. She said, "Slow down! Calm down! Come on in!" She took me to the table and asked, "Are you hungry?" I let her know that I hadn't eaten today. She made me a plate, put it on the table, and she grabbed the phone to call her mom. They argued for a few minutes. I overheard her say, "Mama please just go get my baby out of jail!" After she got off the phone, she lit a cigarette, sat down, crossed her legs, and looked at me. Then she said, "Son, please eat. It will make you feel better and me too." She turned on the radio and Karen White's, "I'd Rather be Alone" came on.

As the music began to play, she began to make her drink. The next thing I know, she was giving me a real show. She began to rock and sway, and she let out a yell. She got up and she began to sing along with Karen. Her performance honestly began to make me feel better too. It made sense to me, because I was used to my mom doing the same thing when she was stressed. It would also put her in a good mood. As the music began to fade, there was a knock on the door. Before she got a chance to get up, the door flew open. It was her mom and her brother. Her brother didn't waste any time sharing his feelings with his sister. He said, " Stop calling Mama begging her to help you with this dead beat ass son of yours! I am sick of you and this shit!!" Day Day's grandma quickly tried to get him to stop. Day Day's mama just sat there quietly with her head down. Meanwhile, I was scared and ready to go now. Day Day's grandma calmed her son down, and she said, "Let's go get my grandson." We all began to get ready to leave, then we heard another knock at the door. This time, it was Leon. Day Day's mom jumped up and screamed, "If it wasn't for your ass! Get out! Both of you get out of my house!" I was speechless! I didn't know what was going on.

We walked outside, and Prince was sitting outside waiting on Leon, because they didn't know if Day Day was home, since they didn't see Leon's car. As we got in the car, it smelled like Brute and cigars. Ironically, Prince had the artist, Prince, playing on the radio. I was thinking, "This is totally not my vibe." As we ventured down the highway, I noticed that Prince was looking at me through the rearview mirror. It looked like he was drooling. He asked, "Where to now?" Day Day quickly said, "The Beat." The Beat was a street near downtown where gay men met other gay men for fun. I remember sitting in the back seat about to cry. I was just ready to go home, but here I am off on another adventure. So much time had passed until my pants were now dry again, but I could still smell the urine scent. I hoped that I was the only one that could smell it. I sat there quietly in the back seat, because I began to feel anxiety in my stomach, and I was feeling dizzy.

The next thing I know, I remember hearing my name being called repeatedly and felt a tap on my leg. It was Leon calling my name. He asked me, "Are you okay?" Apparently, I had either passed out or fallen asleep. I quickly replied, " I am! I was just thinking about what happened earlier." Leon said, "Oh yeah!! You were going to tell me about that. Go ahead and finish." As soon as I mentioned the house on 12th street, I felt the car glide to the side of the interstate. Prince put it in park, turned around with a big smile, and said, "Bitch! Give me that tea! All of the tea!" As I began to spill the tea, Prince said, "This is some sweet tea here." Then he chimed in, "Chile, I told her to stop letting all those bitches stay with her." This made me ask him, "Is that a bad house or something?" Prince said, "No, the owner is sweet as pie. It is just the company that she keeps. There's nothing to be afraid of there." Prince informed us that he needed to run to Mabelvale to drop off a package. I asked him, "Can you drop me off at home?" That just so happened to be near where my mom lived. He said, "Sure."

Once we arrived at my mom's, I quickly noticed that my stepdad's car was gone. I was too excited to see that he wasn't home. As I walked in, Drewdy ran up to me and grabbed my leg. I was so excited to see my little brother. He had to be around three or four then. My mom was in her room smoking a cigarette, having a drink, and listening to Cherrell"s Saturday Night Love. She was just bouncing to the music which indicated to me that she was definitely in a good mood. I started to hear the dog barking in the backyard which meant that my step dad must be returning. I quickly ran into the bedroom and laid on the bed. I was laying there hoping that everything was a dream. I must have dozed off, because I remember waking up to my brother playing a video game, and I could smell cornbread coming from the kitchen. I walked into the kitchen, and my mom was cooking beans with ham hocks and cornbread. She was listening and singing Michel'le's ``Something's in my heart." My stepdad yelled into the kitchen, "Be quiet! You know I am watching my wrestling, Denise!" She started to laugh, but I got pissed! He has some nerve! Right as I was beginning to really get pissed, I heard the phone ring. I looked at the caller id, and it was Mama! My granny was calling and

I quickly grabbed the phone and answered. I asked her, "Can I come over?" She said, "Yes." Then I asked her, "Can Uncle D come get me?" Mama said, "Put your mom on the phone." I handed my mom the phone. She sat down and began to talk to her. I decided to walk into my sister's room. She was watching "*The Five Heartbeats*." Her favorite part of the movie was on. After our favorite song went off, my mom called for us to come eat dinner.

As I was walking towards the kitchen, I noticed a car pulling up. It was my mom's brother, Uncle D. He came in and grabbed a few bites, but he didn't want to stay long because he didn't care for my stepdad either. I had to get in the backseat, because his lady friend, Penny, was sitting in the car waiting on him. I actually liked this one. She was really sweet and kind. Penny had the prettiest smile, her heart was genuine, and she was even able to keep my uncle in line. When we ended up going to her house, they went into her bedroom. While they were in the bedroom, I sat in the living room watching "Video Soul" with her cat, Pussy. The special guest that night was Vanessa Williams. I loved seeing her beautiful smile and those b.e.a-utiful eyes. As time went on, Penny said, "Go to the store and get some kool aid, and you can keep the change."

I was happy because I was going to grab some Baskin Robbins. As I was walking up the hill towards the store, I noticed that two guys were walking towards me. As they got closer, I realized that one of the guys looked familiar. I couldn't figure out where I knew him from, but I knew him. I tried to keep moving past them, but one of the guys called my name. I looked closer to him and I realized that it was a guy from junior high, Anthony. I took classes with his brother, Brian, but I didn't know him that well. However, I did instantly recall him telling other kids that I had sugar in my tank. He asked me, "Do you live over here?" I told him that I didn't. I couldn't help but wonder what was going to happen next. In my head, I asked myself, "Are they about to jump me?" The other guy continued walking away. I explained to him that I was visiting my uncle's girlfriend, and he told me that he was at his cousin's house going over music for church. I said, "Oh yeah, your dad is a Pastor." As he continued to explain to me the music that they were working on, I found my eyes dancing all over his body. Looking at his light complexion, I remembered that they called him, "Red." Red was about 5'10", big hands, big feet, and even his tongue was big. I couldn't help but believe that everything on this man had to be big!!! The more I studied his body, the more I could feel myself growing inside my fruit of loom underwear. As I felt myself growing, I decided to start walking towards the store, and he continued walking and talking with me. We were so wrapped up into our conversation that I didn't even notice that we had made it to the store. We walked into the store, and I began to look at the different kinds of kool aids. While I was looking at the kool aid, Red reached over me to grab some kool aid packets; I can still remember smelling his body. He smelled like outside but it was a good smell. He grabbed a few packets, put them into my hands while looking deep into my eyes, and he said, "These are some good flavors here." I thanked him and started walking to the checkout. After walking out of the store, he said, "Take the kool aid to your folks, and then come over and chill with me." I was surprised that he asked me to come chill with him, because I didn't play video games, but I agreed to come. We walked back up to the apartment, he sat down on some stairs, and said, "I'll wait here until you come back."

When I walked into Penny's house, I was greeted by the aroma of pork chops cooking. They were smelling so good. I almost told Red that I would talk with him later. Right as I was about to say it, my uncle walked out the bedroom with only his underwear on, with holes everywhere. I quickly said, "I will be back. I saw someone outside that I know." Penny replied, "Okay. The door will be open." My uncle quickly said, "Hell naw! He can eat with whoever he goes with." Penny told me not to worry about it. She said, "I got you." I quickly joined Red who was waiting for me on the stairs. We walked to the neighboring apartment complex. When we walked into the apartment, his cousin was laying on the couch asleep. Red led me into the back bedroom. He walked into the bedroom and immediately began to take his clothes off. I was standing there confused! I didn't know what to do. Once his underwear came off, his member fell to his knees. I was scared! I quickly said, "What are you about to do with that?" He said, "Shut up! We aren't about to do anything." He turned me around, took off my shirt, and pulled my back into him. He began to touch my nipple and lick my ear. While he was touching my nipple and licking my ear, he slowly began to pull my pants and underwear off. Then, I felt that machine gun get closer to my body. He then began to grind against my cakes. It felt so good and his musk smelled so good. Out of nowhere I began to moan, because he was playing with both my nipples. Then,

I began to feel an unfamiliar hand grabbing my groin. At first I thought, "Is his dick that big that it has turned into another hand?" Then, another naked body, the guy that was allegedly his sleeping cousin, came around and began to grind on me in the front. He began to rub his member against mine. It felt so good!!! Even though it was a new experience to me, they made me feel so safe until I couldn't get upset. I just enjoyed the moment. They continued to grind against my body while they kissed. That was the night that I fell in love with hunching.

Later that night after eating my pork chops, macaroni and cheese, and sweet ass kool aid, I found myself laying on the couch watching, "*Pretty Woman*." I was so engrossed in the movie that I didn't even notice my uncle walk into the room. He said, "What in the hell are you watching?" He interrupted my favorite part of the movie. Since he was interrupting my favorite part, I decided to act it out for him. I grabbed my two bags and stood in front of him and said, "Do you remember me? I was in here yesterday, and you didn't want to help me? You're on commission, right? Big mistake. Huge one!" I politely walked out of the apartment with my bags in my hands and walked straight to the car.

CHAPTER THREE

As days went by, I began to wonder if Day Day was okay. I didn't have his number, so I decided to call Leon to ask about him. The phone rang twice, and I heard his girly voice answer. We said our hellos, and as I started to ask about Day Day, he said, "That girl will be okay. She stays in trouble." He quickly changed the subject and began to tell me about his love affair with Prince. I heard his line click, meaning someone was calling. I wanted to hang out, but I needed to know about Day Day. Leon clicked back over and said, "I am going to get you. Are you at your Granny's?" I replied, "Yes." As I freshen up, my great granny called, "Can you come see why your Aunt Fanny isn't answering her phone?" I ran across the street to check on her, and I noticed that my uncle's new car was sitting in the yard. I also heard the dog barking. Then, I heard another dog with a deeper voice, and I was wondering, "When did she get another dog?" Her husband's bedroom window was by the front door. He was in his room snoring so loud until I thought there was another dog in the house. Then, I heard a female voice say, "Who is it?" It was my cousin, Pam. She was such a sweetheart. I asked her, "Where is your mom?" She said, "In there watching *Jeopardy*. She doesn't want to be bothered. She was trying to tune Daddy's snoring out." I guess she had taken a few shots of whiskey and a few puffs of her joint. I gave her a hug, and I walked to let my great granny know that she was okay, but she was asleep. As I walked back to my granny's house, I noticed that Leon was pulling up. However, he had two damn queens in the car with him. They were talking loudly and calling each other bitch and girl. I was embarrassed because my Uncle D and his homie were sitting in a car on the side of the house. As I get in the car, both of the queens yell, "Yes God! His face is beat!" We were riding around, and they were doing j-sette moves while we were riding around town. We pulled into a yard to park. At this moment, I still didn't know their names, because they only referred to each other as bitch, and Leon never took the time to introduce us. When we walked into the house, there were three women sitting in the living room reading magazines, and there was this gay guy doing another lady's hair. He was laying it out! It was perfect! He asked, "Who are you? Why are you hanging with these girls? You are young. How old are you?" Once I said my name, he said, "Speak up baby! I can't hear you." After I told him my name, he said, "I am Stacy. Once again, baby what are you doing with these messy girls?" Before I could answer him, he yelled across the room saying, "Bitch calm down! Don't you see my customers here?"

Leon snapped back, "Bitch, don't come for me!" The lady in the chair looked at him and began to shake her head. I could feel my anxiety rising again, because I didn't know what was going to happen next.

Then, one of the guys of the trio told the other two guys, "Come on let's go to Montgomery Ward and boost." I didn't know what they meant. I guess Stacy must have seen the confusion on my face, because he asked me, "Do you know what they are talking about?" To which I replied, "No, I don't." Stacy looked at them and continued by saying, "They should be ashamed of themselves." One of them looked back at Stacy with a stern look and said, "I don't know this little boy, and I didn't ask him to go with us anyway. He looks underage." This prompted Stacy to ask me again, "How old are you?" This time, I responded with, "I am 15, almost 16." Once I said my age, the room stopped and everyone looked at me. Stacy told the three musketeers, "Leave him here. I will take him home." They quickly dashed out the door.

A few minutes passed by and one of Stacy's clients said, "I have a taste for some Sim's BBQ." Stacy said, "That sure does sound good." Then he looked at me and asked, "Have you eaten anything?" He quickly let him know that I hadn't had anything to eat. I also told him, "Being around that crowd made me not even think about eating." He laughed at me and responded, "They aren't my crowd either. Do you know how to drive?" I told him, "Yes." Stacy told me, "Take my car and run up the street and pick up the food for us." I didn't know what to say, because I couldn't understand how he would trust me with his car, and he just met me a few minutes ago. He handed me his car keys and a 100 dollar bill. When he put them into my hand, he rubbed my hand gently and winked at me. Then he said, "My car is a white Mustang. Be careful." I took his keys and the money, and I walked outside to his car. When I turned the ignition, the church music began to pipe out of the speakers. This made me smile, and I began to drive down Roosevelt Highway. When I pulled into Sim's BBQ parking lot, I noticed a truck that looked just like my stepdad's ugly ass green truck. I took a closer look, and I realized that it was him with a female companion. I made myself believe that this woman was one of his nieces, because he had quite a few of them that looked older. When I opened the door, I was welcomed by the aroma of the food. It smelled so good!!! After receiving my order, I couldn't help but think about my stepdad again, because I wanted to know who was riding with him. I knew that I couldn't say anything to my mom, because she thought I was causing problems for their relationship. I quickly shook that thought out of my head and I began to drive by to Stacy's.

On the drive back, I noticed that Leon and two nameless thunder monkeys were on the side of the road, because they had been pulled over by the police. They were all standing behind the car. I was so glad that Stacy rescued me before this happened. I shook my head and continued to drive back to Stacy's. I parked the car, and I headed into his house. While I was walking towards the house, I noticed a guy was sitting on the porch smoking a cigarette. When I stepped on the porch, he looked at me with examining eyes and said, "Which boy toy are you? I see you're driving the Mustang." Before I could even answer, Stacy came outside, grabbed my hand, and led me into the house. Once we were safe inside, he said, "That's my roomie. Stay away from him. You can wash your hands in my bathroom. It's in my bedroom. It's the third door upstairs to the right." I listened to Stacy, and I began to walk upstairs. When I made it halfway up the stairs, I turned around and noticed that his roommate was following me upstairs. I quickly ran into Stacy's room. When I turned around, his roommate was standing at his door staring at me with a smile and his hand was firmly gripping his dick. He slowly walked away, and I began to explore Stacy's room. I instantly noticed that his room was well decorated and everything seemed to be neatly placed. I continued into his bathroom where I noticed a pile of dirty clothes. On the very top were a pair of dirty under-wear with brown streaks in them. I instantly began to turn up my nose, and I remember thinking, "Ugh!!" I stood there in astonishment. Then, I noticed that there was another pair of underwear there too. I couldn't resist, so I kicked them over and they were even worse than the first pair. I quickly washed my hands and darted downstairs.

When I made it back downstairs, everyone was eating and talking about how good the food was tasting. One of the ladies said, "Umm!! Y'all this is some good food!" She sat there eating it with barbecue sauce on her fingers and dripping down her chin. Her reaction excited me, and it made me quickly begin to eat the plate that Stacy had already prepared for me. After a few minutes of enjoying the food, I remembered that I hadn't given Stacy his change from buying the food. I reached in my pocket, and I attempted to hand him his money. He looked at me and said, "No, you can keep it." I didn't argue with him.

I put the money back in my pocket, and I continued to eat my food and listen to the gossip. The ladies were talking about some women from St. Mark Baptist Church. They talked about women sleeping with married men, and they joked about how some of them were even having sex in the church. I was really enjoying the food and conversation, but something told me to look to my right. When I looked to my right, I saw Stacy's roommate peeping around the half opened door. He was looking directly at me. Stacy noticed him looking and threw his shoe at him. His roommate walked from behind the door, and he looked at me and let out this loud bark. His bark must have really tickled the ladies, because it sounded like we were at a comedy club. They were laughing and falling all over the place. Honestly, I started laughing too. I was laughing until I noticed that Stacy was sitting there fuming. His face made me anxious, and I began to shake my leg. Stacy touched me and said, "Stop shaking your leg! Everything is okay. You shouldn't be so gorgeous." He stood up and apologized to the ladies and said, "Let's get back to doing hair."

Hours later, I woke up on the sofa and all of the ladies were gone. Stacy was washing clothes. I was so relieved that he was washing those dirty drawers. I didn't realize that it was so late. I jumped up to start to head out of the door, and he stopped me. He asked me, "Do you want to stay and cuddle?" I smiled and said, "Yes." He grabbed his car keys and said, "Let's run to the store real quick." As we were walking to his car, he handed me his keys for me to drive. He started to ask me questions about my day. When Day Day's name came up, he said, "That boy stays in trouble. We can ride by in the morning to check on him." When we reached the liquor store, we made it just in time. He ran in and grabbed his bottle. On the drive back, he reached over and put his hand on my leg. I sat there confused, because I didn't get excited. I thought for sure when a man touched me that I should get excited and feel my dick begin to grow, but that wasn't what happened this time. I was so nervous. I didn't know if he wanted to have sex. I told him, "I need to get home. I haven't spoken to my grandma all day." He told me that I could use his phone to talk to her. Then he said, "I will give you 100 dollars, if you stay and just cuddle with me tonight." My eyes lit up! I couldn't believe that he was going to give me that much money to spend the night and just to cuddle. I made sure that I told him that I had never had sex, and I was scared to have sex right now. Stacy reassured me that he only wanted to cuddle, and he wouldn't force me to do anything else.

When we arrived back at the house, we were welcomed by some unfamiliar noises. We walked into the foyer and it was pitch dark, and we heard some strange noises coming from the living room. We peeped into the living room, only to find out that Stacy's roommate was on the floor having sex with this guy. Stacy said, "He must have some young boy in there with him." Stacy grabbed me and quickly took me upstairs to his room and closed the door. Stacy took a few shots and took off his clothes. Then, we laid down on his waterbed. We laid there cuddling. When we were just about to doze off, we heard a knock on the door. Stacy said, "Come in." To my surprise, Leon walked into the room. That's when I realized that Leon was the boy that was having sex with Stacy's roommate. Leon walked into the room, and he immediately began to explain to us that the two thunder monkeys had been arrested because they had warrants. He also informed us that his car had been impounded. He asked Stacy to loan him some money to get his car. Stacy jumped up buttnaked with his dick hanging low and said, "You were just downstairs having sex with my roommate. Why don't you ask him for some money?" Leon turned around, slammed the door, and walked out.

The next morning, I was awakened by his phone ringing. I turned over and he was already awake just staring at me. He said, "Good Morning Gorgeous!" I couldn't help wondering how long he had been staring at me. He finally answered the phone, and it was one of his clients. He told her that he would call her later, because he had plans this morning. When he got off the phone, he looked at me and said, "Get a shower! We are going to M M Cohen to go shopping." I jumped up and walked into the bathroom. When I walked into the bathroom, I noticed that his underwear from last night were on the floor, and they had brown streaks too. I just shook my head and proceeded to get into the shower. I lathered up my body and I began to wash my face and head. A few minutes later, I heard the bathroom door open, and I saw the curtain move. The next thing I know, Stacy was standing in there with me. He grabbed me, pulled me to him, and began to rub on my nipples. I didn't know what was going to happen next. I was so scared! I just stood there with my back to him, and I remember feeling a tear fall. Stacy began to wash my back and my body. He rinsed me off, and then he washed his body. Luckily, he didn't try anything sexual. We both got out of the shower, dried off, got dressed, and left the house.

After a few minutes of driving, he pulled into a Waffle House's parking lot. I remember thinking about how hungry I was, and I kept hoping he would buy me some food. We walked into the restaurant and quickly found a booth. Stacy told me to get whatever I wanted to eat. I ordered triple hash browns with some orange juice. I drowned the hash browns in ketchup, and I stirred it up like it was spaghetti. I was so glad to be finally eating something, because I hadn't really eaten in the last few days. My life had been consumed with so many new confusing experiences until I didn't have an appetite. After eating our breakfast, he paid the bill, and we were back on our adventure.

Ten minutes later, we pulled into the University Mall's parking lot. As we walked into the door of the mall, I quickly noticed Frankie's to my left. Frankie's was a restaurant that my family frequently visited when other family members would come to town. The restaurant sold a watered down version of soul food. Now that I think about it, it was like a Cracker Barrel in the mall with lightly seasoned soul food. As we continued to walk, I began to get lost in my thoughts after seeing Frankie's. I started to reminisce on all of the family outings and all of the laughs that had been shared in that restaurant. I could actually hear my aunts gossiping about each other and anything else that they could think about at that moment. I was so lost in my thoughts that I bumped into Stacy. He asked me, "Are you okay? It looked like you were lost in a trance." I assured him that I was good, and I began to share how seeing that restaurant caused me to go down memory lane in my mind.

He smiled and said, "Oh! We can go there one day, and I will treat you to whatever you want, Gorgeous."

We continued to walk through the mall. The first stop was Montgomery Ward. Montgomery Ward was a store that was similar to a Sears. This store had clothes, appliances, home products, and everything that your normal Sears would have on their shelves. Stacy was on a shopping spree! He was looking for things for his apartment, specifically for his bedroom and his kitchen. After an hour or so of shopping, we began to walk to the register with both our arms full of things he bought. He ended up buying a comforter, pots and pans, and pictures for his walls. When we got to the register, the lady looked at us with a big smile on her face, and she began to ring up his items. Then she looked at him and said, "That will be $670.00." He pulled out his checkbook and began to write the check. After handing her his check, she signaled for the manager to come over. This made me really nervous, because I had been with my grandmother many times before when she would write a check for her purchases, and she always just hands them the check and her I.D. That's it! This was really different! Ten minutes later, we were still standing there waiting for them to verify his check for the purchase. The longer we waited, the more I began to think. Then, I remembered watching some other guys earlier that were changing numbers at the bottom of some checks. When they noticed my look of concern, they told me that they worked for the federal government. They assured me that I didn't have anything to worry about. Looking back now, I can't help but shake my head at how naive I was back then. I actually believe that these "girls" worked for the federal government.

Finally, they verified his check and accepted it. Then, we went off to the next store.

The next thing I knew, we were in M.M. Cohen, and he was in hog heaven again! He was running around the store just grabbing clothes without even trying them on. He looked at me and said, "Go ahead and pick out any outfit that you want. I am about to go over here and get some more things." I darted off to look for an outfit. While looking for my outfit, I can still remember wondering, "What is he up to?" However, I didn't allow my wandering mind to stop me from finding an outfit. After several minutes of looking, I found something to wear. It was a pair of Duck Head khaki pants and Duck Head polo style shirt with green and burgundy stripes. I was happy! When we got to the register, I put my clothes down with his things. As soon as I saw him pull out his checkbook again, I walked outside to wait on him. From that day forward, whenever anyone other than my grandmother pulled out a checkbook, I quickly exited the stage!

After about five minutes or so of waiting, he walked out the store with our bags. I felt relieved. We put the bags in the car, and we began to drive away from the mall. A few minutes into our drive, he said, "Oh shit! It's time to head to Day Day's house!" He then looked at me with a very suspicious look, and he asked me, "Have you ever slept with Day Day before?" I told him, "No! I am just worried about him." Twenty minutes later, we turned down the street to Day Day's house. The closer we got to his house, I noticed that there were alot of cars in the driveway, in the yard, and down the street. It looked like they were having a big party. We were hesitant about stopping, but we decided to stop. We parked the car, and before we could even get out of it, a guy walked up to us and said, "Thanks for coming!" We were really confused now. The guy was dark skinned with milk chocolate skin. You could see his muscles bulging through his fitted dress shirt, along with the frame of his body. Stacy asked him, "What's going on? Why are you thanking us for coming by?" The guy said, "I am his cousin, David. All of our family came into town, because Day Day passed away from pneumonia." We both stood there speechless!! I remember thinking, "I knew something wasn't right! I felt it, but none of the others even cared." We continued to stand there and talk to David while listening to him tell us about the events leading up to Day Day's death. Then, a lady walked out with a matted wig on her head. She stood there with her hand on her hip looking at us with a glaring look. She asked David, "How can we help them?" David said, "I got it handled Auntie!" Then with a stern voice she said, "She doesn't want them here." She walked away quickly.

Stacy looked at me, and then he asked David, "What does she mean? Who doesn't want us here?" David informed us that Day Day's mom blamed all of the gay people for his death, and she didn't want us there. He also said, "Please let all of your friends know that they aren't welcomed at his funeral either." We thanked him for talking to us, and we decided to leave. As we were driving away from the house, Stacy suddenly yelled, "Damn!!! He was only 18, and the sickness got him!" His tone was so touching until I could feel his pain too. As we drove back to his house, I couldn't help but think about all of the events that I had seen over the last week. I thought about what happened at the house on 12th street with the guy being stabbed, Day Day being arrested, Stacy and the checks, and now Day Day is dead. It was just too much for my almost 16 year old mind to process. Is this what being gay is like? If so, I don't think I want any part of this madness!!!

After riding around for two hours to clear our heads, we pulled up to this unfamiliar house. Well, it was actually a duplex with a broken screen door. Stacy told me, "This is my good Judy's (the nickname for gay men's close friend) house. His name is Byron." As we walked closer to the door, it miraculously opened without us knocking or buzzing a doorbell. Then, this short dark skinned guy with an Al B. Sure kind of haircut, and a thick mustache that needed to be groomed appeared. Byron looked me over once, and he asked Stacy, "Bitch, who is this little boy?" Stacy introduced me, and Byron gave me a hug and invited us inside. Byron walked to his bar, and began to make them a drink. While Byron was making their drinks, they began to have a conversation. Byron told Stacy, "Bitch, the girls are just going on. They are passing from pneumonia. It's not safe these days to catch a cold. If you hear a cough, and they have a knot on their neck, they are dead people walking." Byron looked at me and said, "Baby these girls ain't right! You are the talk of the town. Please don't let them get a hold of you." I began to think to myself, "This lifestyle is turning me off by the second." Byron and Stacy finished their drinks, and Byron then asked Stacy, "Can we ride to the Bluff?" Stacy objected at first, but then he said, "If we go, you can't be doing any stunts, honey." The next thing I know, we were in the car heading to the Bluff.

It seemed like Byron was waiting patiently for us to get onto Highway 630, because as soon as we made the right turn, he turned around and began to question me. Byron said, "Everyone is trying to find out where you came from." He then asked, "Where did you come from? Who turned you out? Who did you give those goodies to?" I replied quickly, "I haven't had sex yet." Byron looked at me with a very perplexed face and asked, "Are you even gay?" I told him, "I don't know. I have only hunched two people." This made Byron gag! Before he could interrogate me anymore, we pulled into the parking lot of the apartment complex. From the car, I could see five guys on the balcony of this apartment moving their arms and bodies. I later learned they were j-setting. I was hoping that wasn't where we were going. Byron told us, "Come on let's see what these queens are up to today." As we walked closer to the door of the apartment, the guys on the balcony eyes began to follow us. By the time we made our way inside, all of them were already inside of the apartment. We walked into an apartment full of guys... I counted ten, not including us. Before I had a chance to really get acquainted with this new environment, I heard someone say, "Terrell!" I was shocked and scared! I stopped in my tracks to see who knew my name. It was Chris. He was one of the guys from the house on 12th street. He then said loudly, "You are getting around quick!" I was so embarrassed that I decided to walk back outside to the car, but before I could make it to the car, Stacy's roommate pulled up. He had two guys in the car with him. He said, "Hey! Come here lil Roni!" I walked over to the car. He asked me, "Why are you with Stacy?" I replied, "We aren't together. We are just friends."

Before he got a chance to respond, everyone came outside of the apartment. One of the guys said, "Stacy, your little boy-friend is trying to get your roommate now!" Byron then yelled from the car, "Get in the car, because the Bluff girls are messy!" As we were driving away, I began to wonder, "Will I ever make a friend?" We took the 30 minute drive back to Byron's house. When we got there, Stacy said he was too tired to drive, so we ended up spending the night. Stacy was really upset with me, because he thought that there was more going on with me and his roommate. That night, he let me sleep on the sofa, and he slept in the room with Byron.

CHAPTER FOUR

The next morning, I awoke to a house filled with the smell of bacon. I laid there for a minute trying to figure out where I was, when a sharp pain shot through my back. That's when I remembered that I had been sleeping on a sofa at Byron's house. As my eyes began to focus, I noticed that there are three older gay men sitting directly in front of me on an adjacent sofa with their legs crossed. One of the older men looks at me with a cigarette hanging out of his mouth and says, "Who are you?" The second guy looks like the Crypt Keeper from "Tales from the Crypt", and the last guy sat there with his lips poked out and he asked, "Are you even gay?" Honestly, it made me question myself. I began to wonder...*am I was even gay*? After a few seconds of questioning my sexuality, I told them, " I was introduced by Leon." The three guys then said in unison, "Oh Lord!" They quickly asked, "Have you had sex?" One of them yelled, "Speak up honey!" I wanted to snap back with, "You cunt", but I was raised to respect my elders. It was easier to respond to the one with the cigarette, so I only looked at him when I would respond. He was a little calmer and didn't make smart remarks to every answer that I gave them. They asked, "How old are you?" To which I replied, "I am about to be 16." Before they could comment on my age, Stacy walked out of the kitchen, looked at me, and said, "Breakfast is ready. Welcome back! You were out of it last night, and I didn't know where you lived to take you home. Come get something to eat." Stacy led me into the kitchen and told me to have a seat. Then, he began to make my plate for me. While he was making my plate, the older guy that had been sitting with his lips poked out asked him, "Why are you making his plate? Are you trying to get into his pants? Bitch, I hope you end up in jail like the rest!" I started eating, and I looked up and everyone was staring at me! It made me nervous as hell! Luckily, Byron broke the awkwardness when he asked me, "What are your plans today?" I replied with, "I need to get home. Where's your bathroom?" Byron said, "It's down the hall in my bedroom." Once I finished eating breakfast, I quickly walked down the hall to his bedroom. When I walked into his bedroom, I noticed clothes all over the floor. As I walked through the room, I was hoping that his underwear didn't look like Stacy's underwear full of streaks. The closer I got to the dirty pile of clothes, I couldn't resist the urge to look. When I looked, I noticed that he had dirty underwear and nasty socks too. The socks looked like he had been walking outside with just socks on, and all of his underwear were filled with dirty streaks that ran up and down them.

The sight was sickening! I wanted to pee but the toilet was so damn dirty that I walked right back out and asked Stacy to take me home. He told me, "Hold on! I have to clean the kitchen." I decided to take a seat on the sofa with Byron. When I looked at the table, I noticed that the three other guys from earlier, "The Three Supremes", were cutting numbers off of some checks, and they were replacing them with new numbers. I was very curious because the other guys said that they worked for the government when they were manipulating the checks, but I doubted if everyone worked for the government. I gently whispered to Byron and asked, "What are they doing?" He told me, " They are professionals, that is something that you shouldn't pay attention to." I listened to him and remained quiet but I continued to watch with curiosity. Shortly after, Stacy walked out of the kitchen, looked at me, and said, "Come Gorgeous! Let's hit it!" I jumped up from the sofa, and told Byron, "See you later and thank you for letting me sleep here last night."

Once we got in his car, Stacy said, "I need to make a stop." We ended up making a stop at Stein Mart. After a few minutes of shopping, Stacy tells me, "Go get a few outfits for yourself." I know my eyes must have lit up and I darted across the store to the mens section. I looked and looked until I was able to find three outfits that I liked. After I finished picking out my outfits, I found Stacy, and we walked to the register. The lady began to ring up our items, and I noticed that Stacy was pulling out his checkbook again. That was my sign to head out the door, because I didn't want to be there when he wrote the check. I walked outside and stood by his car waiting on him. I looked up and saw Stacy quickly walking to the car. When he got closer, he said, "Yeah, you did right by walking off. Checks are not good! Please don't get involved." That's when I noticed he didn't have any of the items with him. He unlocked the car and said, "Get in!" I couldn't close the door fast enough, because he was already pulling out of the parking space. A few minutes later, Stacy reached over and began to rub my leg. He looked at me and said, "Be careful, these girls are trying to suck the life out of you. They aren't right! My client keeps blowing up my pager. I want you to drop me off at the shop, take my car and wash it, and then grab you something to eat." When we got to the shop, his client was already waiting for him. He got out of the car, gave me 50 bucks and said, "Be careful! Come back in about 2 hours." I took his car to the car wash, and I sat there patiently waiting for them to finish it. When they were done, I handed the guy a twenty dollar bill.

As I was driving away from the car wash, I decided to make a quick stop by my Granny's. Once I made the right on Brown Street, I quickly noticed that my grandmother was standing outside talking to her brother, Bubba, and his wife. I couldn't even get out of the car good before Granny was at the door yelling, "Whose fucking car is this and how did you get those clothes?" She said, "Out of any of them, I know your ass isn't out here stealing boy!" My grandmother was so upset that she just walked back over to her brother before I could even think about an answer. I decided to leave while I had the chance, so I quickly sped off. I spent the next two hours driving around waiting for Stacy to finish. The more I drove, I couldn't help but think about Day Day. I hate that he passed away before I got a chance to know him. I could feel my eyes begin to water as I thought about the possibility that he and I could have been good friends, if not more. Then, I began to wonder if he also had dirty underwear. While I was deep in thought about Day Day, I heard a car horn. I looked to my right, and there was a car full of four gay guys. They motioned for me to roll my window down. I cracked the window to see what they wanted with me. As I was cracking the window, I heard one of the guys say, "Bitch, I didn't know that Stacy had a little boy!" One of them asked me, "Who are you driving Stacy's car?" I didn't say anything. When the light turned green, I hit the gas. I was so glad that it changed. While driving down Broadway, I kept trying to understand how they knew that it was Stacy's car. At the next red light, I saw my stepdad's truck, and I was wondering what he was doing during work hours. Then, I thought to myself, "Maybe I should spend the night at my mom's tonight. It's been awhile since I have done that." When the light turned green, I started back to the shop. When I got there, I noticed that there were three more cars parked. Once I walked into the shop, there were a handful of gay guys just sititng there talking to him. Before I could get in the shop, I heard someone say, "Bitch I'll break your mug!" I looked confused because he looked at me when he said it. I felt so uncomfortable. Stacy saw that I was uncomfortable and asked me, "What do you want to do today?" I told him, " I need to get home to my mom's house." A few minutes later, all of his friends decided to leave. I was so relieved that they were gone. Once they were gone, he looked at me and said, "Chile you are the talk of the Rock! Everyone is talking about you and trying to figure out who you are!" I didn't know if that was a good thing or bad thing. I began to think to myself, "Why are gay guys so messy? They don't even know me. This isn't what I wanted." I could barely think because I was so confused and annoyed. I asked Stacy, "What did I do wrong for people not to like me?" He replied, "You are young fresh meat and your face is beat! Just be yourself and fuck them girls! They have nothing going on for themselves, but needles and dicks. They are only sitting around doing drugs and having sex."

When we pulled up to my mom's house, he handed me a 20 dollar bill. As I was getting ready to get out of the car, he leaned over and kissed me on my forehead. Then, I got out of the car and started walking to the door. As I got closer to the door, I could feel my anxiety increasing! I really didn't want to come here, because I didn't know what kind of my mood my step dad would be in tonight. I didn't have anyone to talk to about how I felt but my great aunts. However, my mom didn't like when I did talk to them, because she thought that made them not like him. When I walk through the door, I see my little brother watching Power Rangers. He leaped up from the sofa, ran over to me, and he began to hug my leg really tight. I decided to join him on the sofa. While sitting on the sofa, I began to wonder, *"Why am I even here? Am I wanted here? Where am I wanted? Where can I go? I feel so lost, confused and unhappy!"* After watching one episode with my brother, I decided to go lay down; maybe this will make me feel better. A few hours later, I was awakened to screaming and my little brother crying. I heard my mom say, "Why are you coming in here with lipstick on? Who is she? What's her name?" My step-dad replied, "Vanessa. Vanessa Williams." Then, I heard a hard bump, and my mom yelled, "Why did you push me into the window you black bastard?" My little brother jumped up and ran into their room yelling, "Stop it Daddy! Stop it!!!" After I heard him say that, I rolled over and tried to force myself back to sleep. While waiting to fall back to sleep, I said to myself, "*I gotta get out of this house!*"

CHAPTER FIVE

The next morning, I woke up to a chilly October morning. The leaves had already begun to turn colors, and it was one of those mornings where the air was cool until you could taste the chill of it. The house seemed quieter than normal. I could hear the clock in the living room ticking, the neighbors' chickens were clucking, and in the distance you could hear the cows. Once I realized that I was probably home alone, I decided that I should take out Jane Fonda's workout tape "*Start it Up*". It always seemed to motivate me to get up and get moving. I rarely have a chance to watch it, because my stepdad always shakes his head whenever he sees me watching it. I walked into the living room and as soon as I motioned to get the video cassette off the big screen floor model tv, I noticed my mom sitting on the couch smoking her cigarette. She motions for me to come join her on the couch. Once I joined her on the couch,

she said, "We need to figure out how to get you back in school."
My whole attitude quickly changed, because I didn't want to
talk about it, and I had dreaded this conversation. I knew that
it was going to eventually come up. I haven't been in school
for almost a year now. When they sent me to Cleveland to stay
with my great-aunt, her daughter forced me to leave prema-
turely by being so rude and ugly to me. She never wanted me
there, and it seemed like she made it her mission to send me
packing as soon as possible. When I returned to Little Rock, I
never enrolled in school. The look on my mom's face told her
seriousness about this conversation, so I decided to just listen to what she had to say. My mom looked at me with a very
serious yet sad face. I could see the tears beginning to form in
her eyes. That's when she asked me the question that I wasn't
anywhere near ready to answer. She looked at me and asked,
"Son, are you gay?" She continued with, "I don't know how
to help you if you don't talk to me. I took you out of school,
and I sent you to live with my aunt because she was a school
teacher. That didn't work out. We noticed that you are always
in the streets with people that we don't know. I tried to hold
my tongue, because I was hoping that this was a phase, and
you would quickly figure it out. Baby, if you are gay, its okay.
You know my cousin was gay. Tirrell was so caring and loving.
Everyone was crazy about him. That's how you got your name.
So if you are gay, it's okay. Just be honest with me, so I can help
you." I sat there confused, because I didn't know how to answer
the question. I was still trying to figure it out myself. My mom
continued by telling me, "When Tirrell died, the whole family
drove up to Chicago for his funeral. We were on our way back

to Little Rock, and we got stuck in a snowstorm. While we sat on the side of the road, I began to feel sharp pains in my stomach. I prayed to God that my baby would be okay. That's when I decided to name you after my cousin. Honestly, you even look like him." After she finished telling me about her cousin, I sat there still unsure how I would answer her question. Luckily, the "*Young and Restless*" theme music began to play, and I was able to escape answering the question this time.

When the first commercial came on, she got up, went into the kitchen, and she put on some beans. I guess she must have taken off work today. A few minutes later, the phone began to ring. I answered it, and my grandmother was on the other line singing an old church hymn, "Blessed Assurance." I sat there on the couch with the phone to my ear, and I listened to her sing the song. She has such a beautiful voice, and her singing always moves me. I said, "Hello again!" That's when she said, "Diddard, what are y'all doing?" I told her what we were doing and she told me to let her speak with my mom. I gave my mom the phone, and they talked for a few minutes. They were talking until my mom heard Victor Newman's voice. When she heard him say, "Victoria", she quickly told her mom, "I have to go! My soaps are back on!" We both sat back on the couch to watch the show. When the next commercial came on, my mom looked at me and asked, "Whose car is that you be driving? I am talking about that white Mustang. How are you getting all of these new clothes? They are too old for you to be around. All they see is a fresh new face and fresh meat! They don't care anything about you. Plus, some guy kept calling here looking for you the other day. His name is DayDay." When she said his name, my heart dropped!!! I couldn't believe that he had been calling me before he died! I didn't know what to say or do. I had to fight back the tears, because I wanted to start crying. However, I didn't even want to think about trying to explain that to my mom. She slammed her hand on the couch and yelled, "Damn it Diddard! Please talk to me! How can I help you?" I told her that DayDay had just passed away before I got to know him. She asked me, "How did he die?" I told her, "I heard he had a bad cold." She lit another cigarette and asked me, "Has anyone in the family ever touched you?" I quickly replied, "No!" As soon as the show came back on, the phone began to ring. She yelled out, "Damn it!" She answered the phone. She said to the person on the other line, "Oh! You'll be here in five minutes?"

It seemed like a second later, someone was knocking on the door. She opened the door, and it was her sister, RiRi. I don't know how she did it, but she always seemed to come around when she was always needed the most. Whenever she came around, we would always talk and pray with her, and we would always be happier when she left. My mom quickly grabbed her by her hand and led her to her bedroom. They closed the door behind her. I was so surprised to see her out driving, because she was due any day now, and she was instructed to not drive her manual shift car.

After a few minutes, I realized that it was going to be a long conversation, so I decided to pop in my Jane Fonda video and move my hips with her! After an hour or so, they both reentered into the living room. My aunt came over to me, gave me a big hug, quoted a scripture, and she said, "You will always be my baby boy! You should come over soon and spend the weekend with my little brother, Shawn." I knew that once she had this little boy in her belly, I would instantly stop being her baby boy. As my aunt was walking out the door, the phone started ringing again! This time, it was my great-aunt, Fanny. I answered the phone. When she heard my voice, she said, "What's the tea Greeta? I want you to come over and help me plan mama's birthday dinner. We are going to do it on Thanksgiving Day, because it is the day before her birthday." I told her, "My mom said she would bring me over after she picks up my little brother from school." My aunt quickly snapped back, "Baby, tell your mom that's okay. I will send your Uncle Duke to get you now. Go ahead and get ready! I will see you in a few."

An hour later, I sat on the couch still waiting for my uncle to pick me up. By this time, I had showered, packed an overnight bag, and I was sitting there patiently waiting. While waiting for my uncle, I kept hoping that my mom didn't revisit the question about me being gay. The longer I sat there, I began to get bored. I decided to do some more workouts with Ms. Jane Fonda. After a few minutes of moving my hips, I heard my mom standing behind me laughing. She shook her head and asked me, "Diddard what in the hell are you doing?" She walked into the kitchen, but she was still laughing hysterically at me shaking my hips. She got back on the phone, and she continued laughing while talking. I sat down on the couch, because I was embarrased!! A few minutes later, she yelled back into the living room and said, "Pack a bag. Duke is about to pull up in a few." Little did she know, I had already packed my bag. I dashed into the den to grab the bag. When I walked in there, the dog began to bark. I instantly felt my chest begin to tighten up, because the dog only barked when he heard my stepdad's truck coming. I heard my mom in the kitchen yell, "Damn! He must have gotten off early!" I walked into the kitchen to wait on my uncle, and my mom asked me, "Do you remember years ago when you guys used to perform En Vogue's songs in front of us? You would be really up there shaking your hips! If you are gay, please let me know so I can help you." I didn't know how to answer the question! I just stood there waiting for my uncle. I didn't know what she wanted me to say. I only felt comfortable telling my great-grandmother stuff, because she always listened to me. However, she would listen and later end up telling all of her daughters what we had discussed. I decided to start holding it in, but it always made me feel so sad. My mom assured me that I was so loved in the family, and they would help me, if I told them. I looked out the window to see what was taking my step dad so long to come into the house. When I looked out the window, I saw him and my uncle talking. They must have pulled up at the same time. I quickly grabbed my bag and darted for the door. I decided it was best to stop them from telling each other a bunch of lies.

I walked past my uncle and stepdad, but neither of them spoke to me. By now, this was normal, so I didn't think anything about it. As soon as my uncle turned his car on, his favorite song began to play. He must have been in a good mood, because he sang right along with it like I wasn't in the car. We drove to my aunt's house without saying a word to each other, but when we pulled into the yard, he decided to start a conversation. Uncle Duke looked at me and said, "I heard you were shaking your hips to Jane Fonda. You must want to look like her? Yo mama and all her sisters think that shit funny, but I don't! You better not let me see you do it!" As he was letting me know how he feels, I saw his daughter, Pam walking to the car with a big smile on her face. Aunt Fanny was in her bed on the phone laughing with her sisters, Sherrie and Bubbles. They sure were tickled! I decided to sit down and get the tea. That's when I learned that I was the tea, because they were talking about me shaking my hips to Jane Fonda. Aunt Fanny said to me, "Get in front of the tv and show me how it is done." I quickly jumped up and started shaking my hips. My Aunt Fanny was describing to her sisters how I was doing it, and you could hear them laughing through the phone. As soon as I got into a motion, Uncle Duke walked in and told my aunt, "Y'all should be ashamed of your damn selves!" That's when her phone must have beeped, because she said, "Let me get Dot in on the conversation too." Dot was her other sister. I wasn't sure why this was the talk of the hour. They said, "Yes, he sure does remind us of Big Tirrell!" This was the first time I had ever heard anyone other than my mom say that I reminded them of my cousin that I was named after. She finally hung up the phone and said, "You can come work at my restaurant when you turn 16 in January." I was so happy. My aunt owned the only African American restaurant in the Heights. I could only imagine how this would be such a good move and experience for me. Most of my family worked there already. My grandmother managed it, my mom worked there, a couple of the cousins worked there too, and my Uncle D ran the kitchen. Whenever I was there eating, I loved watching my family interact with the public, because it was my model for what I should be when I started working there.

When she heard *Jeopardy's* theme song coming on, she told me to hand her a bottle, her ashtray with her reefer, and I knew that was my que to leave out of the room so she could watch *Jeopardy* in peace. She reached over and took the phone off the hook. I gladly walked out the room to join Pam in the living room. I was excited about working at the restaurant. I began to ponder to myself, "*Will this distract me from thinking about being gay? Or will it not?*"

A few short seconds later, I joined Pam in the living room where we sat, talked, and laughed. Pam and I loved to mock different family members. We would get up and act out each character. We loved to mock Aunt Bubbles. We would put our hands on our knees and say, "Oh yeah, I have had both of my knees replaced." We were enjoying laughing and mocking our family members so much until we didn't realize that 30 minutes had passed until Aunt Fanny came out of her room and caught us imitating one of her sisters. That's when she quickly told us, "Y'all better stop mocking my sisters!" Then she started laughing too. Then she told us, "I am going next door to check on mama."

Pam and I sat in the living room for a few minutes until we thought Aunt Fanny had made it to her mom's house. That's when Pam looked at me and asked, "Are you ready?" I already knew what she was talking about. Whenever Aunt Fanny would leave us alone, we would always go into her closet and play with her wigs. I couldn't answer Pam fast enough, because before I could agree, she was already full speed ahead down the hall to my aunt's bedroom. Once we were inside her closet, we would choose wigs that looked like ones that Whitney Houston and Anita Baker would wear. Pam had a small radio that she would bring in the closet with us. I am not sure how it always worked out, but it would generally play songs from either Whitney or Anita back to back and we would take turns lip syncing to each singer with my aunt's wigs. Our lip sync battles were always rigged, because Pam could actually sing. Therefore, she knew how to imitate the singers much better than I did, but that didn't seem to phase either of us. We would just continue to battle each other. One time, I was standing there in awe watching Pam sing, and the unthinkable happened. I suddenly felt a presence standing behind me. At first, I thought it might be a ghost, but when I turned around, I could have fainted! It was Uncle Duke, Aunt's Fanny's husband. He had the most disgusted look on his face. For a moment, I could not understand why he was glaring at me like he was, but then I remembered and I said to myself, "*Fool you still got on that damn wig!!!*" Before he had a chance to say anything to me, Pam began to start crying and screaming, "Daddy! Daddy! I am sorry!" Uncle Duke just shook his head, turned around, and walked back to his room with the disgusted look painted on his face. After he was gone, I looked into the mirror and I asked myself, "*What in the hell am I doing?*"

CHAPTER SIX

Later that evening, I was at my grandmother's house. After my uncle caught me in a wig, I felt it was best that I left. After walking through the house and checking for family members, I realized that I was home alone!!! I quickly darted to my grandmother's closet. Once inside, I put on her silk tight dress, her red pumps, and her fur coat. I loved the way the dress fit so nicely on my grandmother that I couldn't resist trying it on. After I had put on all her clothes, I decided to walk out of the closet and look at myself in the mirror. I stood there looking at myself in amazement, because I looked good in the dress. I started trying to figure out which gospel song I would play so I could lip sync, dance, and shout to it like I was a good church woman. Before I had a chance to select the song, I heard a door slam in the house. I panicked! I tried to take the dress off before whoever made it to my grandmother's room. That's when I heard my uncle yell, "Mama!" Before I could finish taking off the clothes, the bedroom door swung open and my uncle stood there with this shocked look on his face. Then, he burst out laughing!!!! My uncle looked at me and said, "You remind me of my cousin, Terrill." He walked out the closet and slammed the door. Then I heard the front door slam. A few seconds later, the front door opened and slammed again. I figured it was my grandmother this time, so I decided to finish trying to get out of the dress. This time, I ripped it trying to get it off. That's when my grandmother's bedroom door flew open, and it was her and one of her boo thangs that stood there looking at me. There I stood in front of my grandmother and her boyfriend in her silk dress trying to get it off! I could have died three deaths! The look on my grandmother's face was embarrassed, angry, and confused! She had her lip poked out like she was mad as hell too! She looked at me and said, "Damn!" Before she could say anything else, the phone began to ring. She ran to the phone, looked at the caller ID, and she immediately unplugged the phone. They both walked out and she slammed the door. After her reaction, I had to check the caller ID, because I was sure the phone was for me which caused her to unplug it. I looked at the caller ID, and it said, "R White". That was my grandmother's other man's name.

After they were both gone, I was finally able to get out of her dress and get back into my clothes. That's when I laid down on her bed and began to cry. I couldn't believe it! I had been caught three times in one day by three different family members in either women's clothing or a wig. I lied there and cried for at least 20 minutes or so. When I was finally able to pull myself together, I decided to walk over to my great grandmother's house, because I hoped she had cooked dinner. When I made it outside the house, my grandmother and her boyfriend were standing beside his car. It looked like she was trying to hurry him to leave, but he wasn't budging. I continued on my journey to my great-grandmother's. When I put one foot in her yard, I looked to my right, and I saw this short, two door convertible Mercedes sitting at the stop sign. The car was a nice champagne color. I only knew one person in town with this car, and sure enough, it was R. White!!! I continued to the porch and I sat down behind the wall to watch this one play out. While I was sitting there waiting, I heard a voice behind me whisper, "Terrell." It was my great-grandmother. She decided to watch the show too. Apparently, R. White had been calling her house looking for my grandmother too. I didn't know how my grandmother was going to handle this situation. I walked into my great-grandmother's house, and we both decided to watch safely from her window. That's when the phone began to ring again. Damn! The phone always rang when something good was going on! I ran to get it! I answered the phone, and I said, "Hellllllloooooo!" That's how my great-grandmother would always answer it, and it made my aunts angry because they said I was mocking their mother. When my aunt heard it, she quickly said, "Stop mocking my mama!!!" I started laughing and passed the phone to my great grandmother. While they were talking, I decided to go take a seat on my great-grandmother's bed. When she saw me sitting there, she yelled, "Terrell! Get off my bed! It is for laying not sitting! Plus you got on your britches!" She went back to her ironing board to iron her linen while she continued laughing and talking with her daughter. A few minutes later, I heard my grandmother walking into the house singing her favorite hymn. She was singing, "This is my story, this is my song……" As soon as she looked at me, she stopped singing and poked her lip out. Then she yelled, "Stay out of my closet!" Then she said, "Come on! Let's go! I need to get my hair done while I can catch Mrs. D." As we tipped down the street, she stopped at Lassie's Fish to get her and Mrs. D. some food. After we finished grubbing, my grandmother sat in the chair, and Mrs. D began to scratch her head. That's when they began to gossip in code. I could hear them, but I couldn't understand what they were saying. Then, I heard Mrs. D. say, " What!!!! Not in you and Fanny's closets ?" Then she asked my grandmother, "Chile, does he be in his mama's closet too?" My grandmother told her, "Naw!!! Ain't shit in there that he wants to try on. The only time that he goes in there is when he is spying on that sorry ass man that my daughter married!" Mrs. D asked, "Girl, what is going on there?" My grandmother told her, "Chile, we will save that for another time." That's when my grandmother began to tell her about what happened with her men earlier that afternoon. She said, "Chile, this is what I need to be telling you about! I know I told you about us catching that boy in there in my closet, but I didn't tell you this part of the story. After we went outside and Ernie was getting ready to leave, that damn R. White's ass showed up unexpectedly." "What did you do chile?" asked Mrs. D. My grandmother told her, "Girl, I have both of them niggas in check!" They both burst out laughing loudly! They continued with this banter until it was time for us to leave. As we were leaving out the door, Mrs. D. grabbed me and said, "It was good to see you honey! Just know that you are loved!"

Early the next morning, I woke up to an empty house. I decided to scroll through the caller ID. As I scrolled through, the phone began to ring, and it was R. White. I answered the phone and he began to ask me questions. I quickly told him, "I haven't been here, so I don't know. She's at work." R. White then said, "I saw you yesterday with your nosy great grandmother in the window. Tell you what, I will buy you a brand new moped." I don't know why I believed this man, but I did! The next thing you know, I was telling him all of my grandmother's business. Once he thought I had given him enough information, we ended the phone call.

As soon as I put the phone back on the hook, it began to ring again. When I answered the phone, I heard someone with a raspy voice say, "Terrell." It sent chills through my body, because I didn't know who it was talking to me, because he took a long pause and only breathed into the phone. Then, he began to talk again. That's when I realized that it was Red. He said, "I have been calling you for days." I didn't know if he was lying or telling the truth, because I hadn't seen his number on the caller ID. However, someone could have been deleting it. He asked me, "What are you doing?" I told him, "I am waiting for the *Young and Restless* to come on." He then asked, "Are you alone?", to which I replied, "Yes!" As I sat there listening to his voice, my body began to tremble with excitement. Then, I heard a little noise that sounded like a cat coming from under the bed. It sounded like a cat that was screaming for help. After a few seconds, I thought it might be my little cousin, Lil Don.

He had a tendency to hide somewhere and listen to my conversations. Then, I realized that it was my great-grandmother calling my name from across the street! I dropped the phone and ran to her house, because I didn't know if she was hurt or had fallen down. When I got to her, she was already standing in the driveway. She asked me, "Why is the line busy? Are you over there running up her phone bill?" I assured her that I wasn't running up the bill. That's when she told me to go up the street to the store and buy her some Pet milk and vanilla extract. After I grabbed her money, I ran back to the phone but the closer I got to the phone, I could hear the phone beeping letting me know that he had already ended the call. When I tried to call him back, his line was busy. I tried a few more times, but it stayed busy. That's when I heard my great-grandmother yelling my name again like a cat in distress.

A few minutes later, I was walking up the street to the store for my great-grandmother. While taking this short walk, I began to think, "*Who keeps deleting the caller ID? And why are they deleting it?*" I was deep in thought until I heard Missy Elliott's "Minute Man". It was blasting from this car that was driving up to me. As it got closer to me, I noticed that it was a white BMW 3 series full of guys dressed with long wigs, jewelry, and women's clothing. As they drove past me, they all waved at me and screamed, "Hey boy!!!" They were all dressed like they had been in their mother's closet. I couldn't understand how I kept getting caught in closets, but they were clearly rummaging through some woman's closet without getting caught. When I made it to the door of the store, I noticed the pay phone, so I decided to give Red another call, but it was still busy! After no answer, I quickly gathered the items she wanted and purchased them. Then, I walked briskly back to deliver them, so I could get back to the phone and call Red.

After I had delivered the items to my great-grandmother, I waited until she started cooking her famous blackberry cobbler. As soon as I heard the dishes moving in the kitchen, I quickly ran and grabbed her phone. I tried to call him once, but it was busy. When I began to try the second time, I heard a thump in the kitchen like someone was hitting something with a fly swatter. Then, my great grandmother yelled, "Terrell you better not be making any long distance calls on my phone!" I quickly replied, "No, I am not!" After he didn't answer the second time, I decided to take the 11 block walk to his house. On my walk, I kept thinking about the queens in the car, my family catching me in the closets, and so much more until the minutes it took to walk those blocks just flew by.

Twenty minutes later, I could see his house in the distance. The closer I got to his house, I noticed there was a very familiar car parked across the street at the church. At first, I couldn't remember where I knew the car from, but the closer I got to his house and the church, it finally dawned on me. It was the same white BMW series that drove past me earlier when I was walking to the store. I began to feel a nervousness coming over me. I didn't want them to see me, so I decided to take the alley behind his house back to my grandmother's. The further I walked down the alley, I began to hear some moaning and groaning. The noises were so intense that they began to make me a little aroused, and I felt my member growing. The more I walked into the alley, the louder the moans and groans grew.

Then, I noticed the two figures in this corner by this tool shed. As I looked closer, I realized that it was Red and some other guy masuturbating. Red had his hands on the other guy's penis, and the other guy had his hand closely wrapped around Red's. When it registered what was going on, I began to feel rage in my body! I couldn't understand. I began to ask myself, "*Why isn't he with me right now? What am I doing wrong? Am I not enough?*" I decided it was best that I leave before they noticed me, so I began the walk back to my great-grandmother's house.

When I reached the family's street, I saw my cousin ,Vinny washing her brand new red Sunfire that my great-grandmother cosigned for her to purchase. When she noticed me walking down the street, she said, "Hey Diddard! What were you doing in Aunt Fanny's bobbed wig singing Whitney Houston?" Then, she began to just laugh and laugh. She laughed so hard until she almost slipped on the soap that was running off her car. We talked a few more minutes while she finished washing her car. When she was done, she began to get ready to leave. I asked her, "Where are you going? Can I ride with you?" She said, "Sure, I am going to take granny to Sears to buy her some linen. Aunt Janice sent her some money." It felt good going to the mall with some people that I could trust. I didn't have to worry about them trying to buy stuff with fake checks.

Once we got to the mall, Vinny quickly found a cute gadget that she wanted for her new car. She asked, "Granny can I have this please?" My great-grandmother smiled and said, "Yes baby!" Then my great-granny looked at me and asked, "Diddard, do you want some socks and bloomers?" I was standing there in disbelief. I thought to myself, "*Wait! She gets*

a shiny new gadget, but I can only get some socks and drawers?"
Then, I quickly remembered that between my cousins and I,
we were always losing some socks. I told great-granny, "Yes, I
want some socks." She smiled and pointed for me to go grab
some. When I made it back to the line to put the things on
the counter. That's when Vinny told us, "I need to go to the
restroom." I watched her as she walked away, and that's when I
noticed that the cashier was watching these two gay guys. They
were a few aisles over in housewares. Their behavior looked
very suspect, even to me. Then out of nowhere, they began
to run towards the exit door. They ran through the door full
speed with arms full of things like toaster ovens, mixers, etc. I
looked out the door and to my surprise, it was the white BMW
again that they were running towards. The security guard
started running after them. The guy driving the car must have
realized that the security guard was going to catch them before
they made it to his car, because before they had a chance to
make it to the car, the car suddenly sped off. The next thing I
know, I was watching the queens chase behind the car, and the
security guard chased them. Unfortunately for the gay guys,
the car left them and they had to deal with their consequences.
As they walked back in the store with the security guard, I realized that I had seen them before at the house on 12th street.
While they continued their embarrassing walk past everyone,
my great-grandmother looked at them, shook her head, and
said, "Po thangs!" Vinny finally returns from the restroom,
and I tell her, "Girl you have missed the action." As we walked
to the car, my great-grandmother and I took turns telling her
about what she had missed. Vinny said, "What! I missed all of

that?" Great-Granny looked at us and asked, "Do y'all want some KFC?" We both smiled and said, "Yes."

On the drive to the KFC, I remembered that we would pass the house on 12th street. As we drove by the house, I noticed that the white BMW and a Uhaul was parked in the driveway. They must be moving. Then, I thought, *"Oh, they were trying to steal some houseware stuff for their new place."* We continued to KFC and bought our food. When we got home, all three of us sat down and began to eat. I sat there eating and laughing at my great grandmother smacking on her food. Then, the phone began to ring. I loved answering her phone, because I never know who is going to call. I jumped up and Vinny did too. We both raced to answer the phone first. I snatched it up and said, "HELLLLLOOOO!" I heard my great Aunt Phoneix say, "Why are you mocking my mama and why are you in my sister's closet?" I didn't know how to answer the question, but I did know that out of all of the closets, I would have rather been in her closet or Aunt Doll's. Both of them could dress! They were really fashionable, and I could only imagine what I could have tried on in either of their closets. Next time, I will go rummaging in hers!

CHAPTER SEVEN

The next morning, I am awakened by a knock on the door. I laid there a little longer waiting on my grandmother or someone to answer the door. After a few minutes of knocking, I decided to go answer it. When I opened the door, I couldn't believe my eyes! It was Red! I wanted to pinch myself to make sure that I was awake, but I could tell by the chill on my face that it wasn't a dream. I wanted to be happy to see him, but all I could see was him and that guy caressing, kissing, and jacking each other behind the shed in the alley. Red asked me, "Are you alone?" I replied, "Yes, I am alone." The next thing I know, he closed the door behind him, he pulled my body into his, pulled my shirt over my head and off, and it began to feel like my body was melting. I led him into my granny's bedroom. He seductively pushed me on the bed, and I landed face forward on my granny's bed. Then, he began to massage my body. He started with my shoulders and slowly began to massage my back down to my butt cheeks. He paused for a second, then he continued all the way down to my feet. Red began to kiss me tenderly on my back, and he worked his way down to my butt cheeks. I didn't know what to do! I had never felt this kind of pleasure before. Before I knew it, I began to faintly moan with pleasure. Right when he began to kiss me more passionately and I began to moan more, I heard some giggles coming from underneath the bed. At first, I thought I was imagining it, but that was quickly dispelled when my little cousins, Lil D and Damiere, slithered from beneath the bed, jumped up, and they ran giggling out of the bedroom. I couldn't believe my eyes! Where did they come from? Red didn't care anything about them or what just happened, because he continued his mission of pleasing my body.

Red really knew what he was doing. I was such a newbie to this, but I could still tell that Red wasn't. After a few more minutes of him kissing my body, the phone began to ring. I ignored it at first, but Red finally encouraged me to answer it. When I answered it, it was Leon. Leon began to tell me about a rumor that he had heard about me. Leon said, "Bitch! I am hearing that you are making your rounds!" I couldn't believe what my ears were hearing. I hadn't been doing anything. I couldn't barely focus on what he was saying, because Red had started taking off his clothes. By this time, he was down to his underwear, and he began to suck my toes. That's when I told Leon, "I am not sure how the rumor got out, but it's a lie! I have to go!" I hung up the phone, and when I turned around Red was standing in front of me completely naked. That's when I remembered that he had a python between his legs! I laid there staring at it in amazement. Red looked at me, looked down at his penis, and he said, "Are you afraid of this little thing? You shouldn't be!" I quickly said, "Yes!" He looked at me with a smile, and began to put his clothes back on. As he was putting on his shirt, he said, "I have to go." After we both were dressed, I decided to walk him out.

When I opened the door, the porch was full of my cousins and their friends! They all just sat and looked at us without saying a word. Once Red had walked off the porch and began to walk down the street, I turned around to walk back into the house. As I was closing the door, I could hear all of my cousins and their friends begin to laugh and giggle. I ignored and I continued back in the house to watch my daily soap opera, "*Young and the Restless.*" I was just getting comfortable when I heard a car's horn blowing. I looked out the window, and it was Leon's car. I walked outside to speak to him, and he said, "Get in the car." I couldn't close the door completely before his friend, Chris, turned around from the passenger seat and he said, "Bitch, we hear you are getting around snacking with everyone!" I was confused! I asked him, "What is snacking?" He then informed me that snacking was when you were having sex with people. That's when Leon pulled off with me in the back seat. I didn't have time to lock the door or anything. I wasn't going to let this rumor continue without defending myself. I told them, " I haven't been having sex with anyone. I have only hunched with two guys." Leon said, "That's not what we are hearing. They said that you are hanging out with a lot of older guys and you must be having sex with them." I quickly said, "That's not true!" We went back and forth for a few minutes. I felt like I was in the backseat with my mom and dad, and they were grilling me about not doing my homework or something.

A few minutes later, I looked up and we were pulling into the driveway of the house on 12th street. My stomach began to sink, and I began to feel nauseous. I didn't know what was going to happen next. I took a quick survey of the yard, and I saw that there were two cars there and the uhaul that was there the other day. Leon and Chris began to get out of the car. Leon noticed that I wasn't making any attempt to get out of the car. That's when he said, "Come on child! No one is going to bother you." I slowly began to open the door and get out of the car. When I closed the door, I looked up and saw two queens emerging from the house. As they walked past us, they said, "Heeeeeeey!" Then one of them looked at me and said, "What are you doing with these two trouble makers? Are they having you?" Here we go again with another word that I haven't heard before. I asked him, "What is having you?" He said, "Child, are you snacking with them, having sex, or hunching? You know what I mean." I told him, "No, I have only been hanging out with them." He said, "Tell me anything!" I was so confused! I began to ask myself, "*Why does everyone think that I am sleeping with anyone that they see me talking to?*" The older queen said, "Just be careful! They are salty! I am Granny!" The other guy finally speaks and he says, "I am Devon. I was Day Day's best friend." Devon wasn't as old as granny. He was only 19 which was just a few years older than me at this time. Devon continued with, "Day Day told me about you. He said you were very sweet and innocent." That made me feel a little better, and I did feel more comfortable now, because someone knew I was innocent.

When we walked into the house, it was full of very flamboyant and femine guys. They were all dancing, but I hadn't seen guys dance like this before. It almost looked like voguing but it was slightly different. I asked Granny, "What are they doing?" He told me, "They are j-setting!" I didn't understand, but that answer was good enough for now. I noticed that a few guys were staring at me. It made me uncomfortable, so I decided to go to the bathroom. I asked Leon, "Where is the bathroom?" He pointed to the door. I walked over to the door, and when I opened it my mouth dropped! The bathroom was filled with dirty clothes everywhere, and I could see that all of the dirty underwear were full of streaks. I couldn't believe that all of these guys didn't know how to clean themselves! I decided to quickly use the toilet and go out of there. As soon as I began to use the toilet, I heard the door slowly opening. I turned around and it was Stacy's roommate. I didn't know what to do! I was scared as hell!!! He closed the door behind me and began to look at me like I was a delectable piece of Popeyes chicken. He walked towards me and pulled my body into his. The next thing I knew, he had dropped his pants and underwear to the floor. I looked down and all I could see was big shit streaks in his underwear. I began to feel sick to my stomach. He pointed at his little member and said, "Touch it!" I told him, "No! I am good! I am just chilling." The next thing I knew, the door flew open and Granny, Devon, Leon, and some tall lanky guy were standing in the doorway. They instantly began to yell at him and tell him to leave me alone! He pulled up his pants, looked at me, and he walked up to me. Then, he licked my nose and began to walk out the room flicking his tongue at me. Granny smacked him in the face as he exited the bathroom.

When we walked back into the living room, it was like time had stopped! Everyone was standing still looking at us, and the music wasn't playing anymore either. That's when one of the guys looked at me and yelled out, "Oh my God! Look at the mug! Your face is beat and you're so innocent!" As I looked around the room, I noticed that everyone was looking at me. Granny must have looked around the room too, because he said, "That's a damn shame! All y'all are looking at him and drooling like vampires! You better not bite into him and spread shit!" I decided to find a seat at the table. Once I sat down, this tall lanky guy came and sat beside me. I later learned that he was the homeowner. His personality was similar to mine. He was quiet and laid back like me. As time would go on, I would spend more time with him because of our similarities and he made me feel comfortable. Then, he let out a goofy laugh and asked, "What are you doing with Leon and Chris? Are they both having you?" I quickly said, "No, they aren't having me. I don't even know Chris that well. I just met him." He said, "You are hanging around him, so yall must be having!" I could feel myself beginning to get upset! I raised my voice slightly and said, "I am not having him!" That's when I felt someone pulling on my arm. I looked up and it was Devon. He motioned for me to follow him, and he led me to one of the bedrooms. When we got to the door of the bedroom, I noticed that the tall lanky guy was walking behind us too. He walked in and closed the door. He then introduced himself to me. He said, "I am Big Dane." He immediately walked over to the radio and turned it on. When he turned it on, Sadé was playing. That's when things began to get interesting!

Once he heard her singing, "There must have been an angel…." He walked into his closet, grabbed a gold sheet that he wrapped around him to look like a dress, and he also grabbed a towel that he wrapped around his head to look like a wig. Then, he began to lip sync to the song while swaying from side to side. Devon quietly took a seat and began to watch him like he was watching a movie. I, on the other hand, was confused! I couldn't understand why he was doing this, and what did this have to do with me? I just sat there in bewilderment. I was so glad when the door opened, and Granny walked into the room. Granny thanked them for rescuing me from the guys in the living room. He said, "Baby, don't let the girls in there make you salty like them. Just ignore them and don't have sex with any of them in that room! That's the best advice I can give you at this point." By this time, Big Dane has finished his song, and he has started to put his costume away. I began to look around the room, and I noticed another pile of dirty clothes with dirty underwear, or as my great-grandmother Julia would say, "bloomers." I began to think, "*Maybe it's the ones with the dirty bloomers that I should keep an eye on.*" Granny looked at me and Devon and said, "Come on, let's go by my sister, Byron's house. He has a roast on." As we were walking out of the bedroom, I began to feel like Big Dane might be one of the good guys. He might just hang around the wrong people. That's when I thought about those dirty bloomers again, and I wondered, "*Is he really one of the good guys?*" As I was about to walk through the door, Big Dane wrote his number on a sheet of paper, handed it to me, and said, "Here's my number. Let's keep in touch. I am not out to get you." Granny looked at me, smiled, and said, "Yes, she's a good person. You should take her number." When we made it back to the living room, we noticed that Chris and Leon had left. Granny looked at me and said, "It's a damn shame that salty ass Leon left you here without even saying anything!"

When we walked outside the house, we noticed that everyone was outside standing around the Uhaul talking. Granny asked, "When are yall turning back in that hot Uhaul?" One of the guys said, "We are going across the river tonight to the punk bar, so we will return it tomorrow evening after church." I thought to myself, "*I hope they don't plan on driving it to church.*" Again, Granny must have been thinking the same thing, because he began to fuss at them about keeping the Uhaul for so long. He said, "Girls yall need to stop renting or stealing these damn Uhausl and driving around in them like they are rental cars for days! That's a damn shame!" I couldn't believe my ears. Are they really doing that? Granny motioned for us to leave, and all three jumped into Devon's car. As we were driving away, I looked back at the house, the Uhaul, and the queens standing around it, and began to wonder, "*Is this what being gay looks like?*"

CHAPTER EIGHT

Twenty minutes later, we pulled up to Byron's small duplex. This duplex looked very familiar to me, but I couldn't necessarily remember who lived here. It was a white, two door duplex, and when we walked up to it, it almost looked like a small forest was to the right. His neighbor to the right was an older white woman that had flowers everywhere. The closer we got to the house, we were greeted by the aroma from the pot roast, and we could hear Lisa Stansfield's "Been around the world..." When it got to the part where she was singing, "I can't find my baby...", Granny began to dance and swing a little. After we fought our way through the mini forest, we made it to his door, and Granny reached through the broken screen door to unlock the door. While Granny was unlocking the door, I realized that the music was actually coming from his neighbor's house. When we walked into the house, we were greeted by Byron with a glass in his hand. You could tell he had been drinking heavily, because the alcohol oozed from his pores. Granny and Devon tried to introduce us, but Byron quickly said, "Oh child, I already know him. He's been here before with Stacy." Granny and Devon didn't say anything, but they both looked at each other and me with a surprise look. After they had reintroduced me to Byron, we all walked to his living room to have a seat on his lumpy couch. The closer we got to the couch, I noticed that he already had some people over there. It just so happened to be two of the guys that I had seen earlier at Stacy's house. They were two of the trio that I had seen before. After we sat down, they sat there with their legs crossed, one had a cigarette in his hand, and the other one had his lips poked out. When I realized that I had met them before, I said, "Hey! How y'all doing? Where is your other friend?" The guy with the cigarette replied, "He is at home with a boil on his ass." The other guy quickly said, "I see you are making your rounds, honey! Child, y'all know Miss Portia (a legendary drag queen in Little Rock) died last night, and they say that Curtis is in the hospital down there in Pine Bluff. " The other guy continued with, "He doesn't have anyone to check on him either. It's sad how we are all leaving here slowly but surely." I didn't understand what he meant by, "We are all leaving here slowly but surely." However, I know this really made me question more if this gay lifestyle was for me.

Out of nowhere, Prince C just walked into the house without knocking or anything. He said, "Bitch, I heard you were cooking! Fix me a plate. I got a trade in the car waiting. He thinks I am checking on my grandma, so I need to make it quick ." I was so scared for Prince C, because he was always with trade (straight men that have sex with guys on the low). When Byron got up to fix his plate, he looked at me and said, "I hope you are taking care of yourself, because I see you are getting around. You should be cool with this clique here." That's when we heard a door close down the hall. Devon and Prince C jumped! They both said in unison, "Bitch, who you got here?" Byron replied, "It's just Taylor. Calm down girls!" Again in unison they said, "Taylor?" Byron told them not to get all excited! Granny said, "Oop! Prince C you better not!" Prince C then looked down the hallway and he began to bark like a dog, "Ruff Ruff!!!" I kept wondering to myself, "*Who is Taylor? Why won't he let us see who he is*?" Byron returned with Prince C's plate, and he walked to the door. As he was opening the door to leave, we heard the horn of a truck, and I saw the glimpse of a uhaul through the window. Prince C said, " Chile, those stunt queens are still riding in that uhaul." We all chuckled as he closed the door behind him.

After the door was closed, Devon said, "Grandpa West told them about keeping those hot trucks for so long!" That made me wonder, "*Do all the gay people ride around in uhauls*?" Byron walked into the kitchen, and he began to make a plate for all of us. Once he had given us all our plates, he made another one and took it to his secret guest that was down the hall. Before I could get into the food, I remembered that I needed to let my mom know where I had disappeared to this time. I asked Byron, "May I please use your phone?" He replied, "Sure. It's over there by the door on the end table." I walked over to the phone, and I dialed her number. The phone only rang twice before she picked up. As soon as she heard my voice, she yelled, "Where the hell are you? You need to bring your ass home now!" I quickly said, " I am about to eat but I will get someone to bring me home as soon as I finish eating." I knew I had to eventually go home, but I wanted to procrastinate as long as possible, because I didn't know what kind of mood my stepdad would be in when I got there.

I joined the rest of them at the table, and I began to eat. After a few bites, I noticed that Byron was staring at me. He said, "You are such a beautiful young man. You are fresh! Please keep it that way." This seemed like the perfect time to tell them about what I was feeling and thinking. I looked at all of them and I began to pour out my feelings. I said, "I see people are talking about me. I haven't had sex with anyone. I am just curious about this lifestyle, but I am beginning to see that it's not a cute one." They all chuckled. Then, the phone began to ring. Byron answered the phone, "Hello! What!!!!! Bitch nah! I will hit you back later!" Byron hung up the phone, and he walked back to the kitchen with a sad face. He looked at us and said, "Ray Ray died." All three of them suddenly had such a sad look on their faces. Granny just dropped her head in his hands and said, "Lord, he was only 18!" I couldn't believe my ears! "*He was only 18? Why are so many young guys dying*?" I asked them, "May I please use the bathroom to wash my hands?"

When I got to the bathroom, I shut the door behind me, and I quickly checked my bloomers to make sure that I didn't have any streaks. Luckily, they were clean. That was such a relief! After checking my bloomers, I looked around the bathroom, and I saw a dirty clothes hamper. I began to wonder,

"*Are there some dirty bloomers in there with streaks*?" Before I reached for the lid, I noticed a few medicine bottles on the counter that looked like the bottles that I had seen at a few of the other guys' houses. My great-aunts Fanny and Bubbles had a lot of medicine bottles in their houses, but none of theirs looked like these bottles. I couldn't help but wonder, "*What are these? Is this medicine making them all mess in their bloomers*? Then, I heard a knock on the door that almost made me streak my bloomers! I quickly shouted through the door, "I am coming!" As I opened the door, the bedroom door across the hall closed. When I walked back into the living room, Byron was on the phone talking to someone named Pumpkin. From what I could tell from the conversation, Pumpkin must live with this Daddy West that everyone keeps talking about how mean he is when he gets upset. The more they talked, it was clear that Pumpkin and a few other guys lived with Daddy West, and they were taking care of his condo downtown, but they didn't pay the electricity bill and the electricity had been disconnected. Byron told him, "Baby, when my good sister comes home, he is going to catch a case!" From what I had been told, Daddy West would get a credit card number and fly home immediately when something goes down. I will make sure that I don't get in his path.

I decided to go see what the other guys were doing at the kitchen table. When I walked up to the table, I quickly noticed that they had some checks spreaded on the table. I sat close to them, because I wanted to know what they were doing with these checks. As I looked closely, I noticed that they were changing the numbers on the checks. I thought to myself, "*I know not to ever go in a store with these two characters, or people riding around with uhauls and dirty bloomers.*" Byron called my name. When I answered him, he said, "Guess what! Chicken butt!" I replied, "Guess why! Chicken thigh!" Everyone started laughing! Devon stopped the room from laughing when he said, "One day this week, I am going to ride to Pine Bluff to check on Curtis. I am going to ask Prince C and Lee to ride with me." Granny said, "It's sad that the girls be going to the hospital, but they don't come out." As I am taking all of this in, there's a knock on the door. Byron yells through the door, "The roast is gone!" Then, the door slowly opens, and a tall dark, slender guy with long hair and extremely long nails walks in. I thought, "*How in the hell did he open the door with those long nails?*"

As he closes the door behind him, he yells, "Hey everyone! Who is that in the car with Prince C? They are down the block fussing in the car!" Granny replied, "Honey, some dirty bird!" I looked at Devon with a confused look and asked, "What's a dirty bird?" He told me, "Dirty birds are salty guys that we call trade. They sleep with man, woman, or anything that walks or crawls. We call them dirty birds." Then he sat next to me, looked at me, and he asked, "And who do we have here? Are you gay? How old are you?" I looked at him and asked, "How old are you?" He said, "I am 17. My name is Shay." I told him, "I am Terrell but they also call me Diddard!" Shay looked at me with a smile and said, "Oh, you're the one that Leon brought out of the closet." He shook his head and said, "You're already a superstar. The girls across the river have heard about you." I quickly said, "What the fuck?" Granny reassured me by saying,

"Honey, that's not always a bad thing." Shay reached inside his bag to get some gum, and I noticed that he also had one of those bottles of medicine in his bag. I couldn't help but notice that Shay's face was dried out. I looked around the room, and I realized that Byron's face is also dried. Shay doesn't look like he eats much. I found myself thinking, "*Poor thing! He really needs to eat!*"

My daze in her purse was broken when we began to hear footsteps coming down the hall. We all stopped what we were doing and fixed our eyes on the hallway to finally see who this mystery man was. I sat there with anticipation. The next thing I know, my eyes were beholding a work of art. Taylor stood about 5'11", muscularly built, bowlegged, red boned, with juicy, kissable lips, and he had a very distinguishable mole on his neck. He walked into the room, and he scanned the room. After he had scanned the room, he looked back at me. Granny noticed that he was staring at me, so he quickly said, "Oh, that's Diddard." The guy looked at her and laughed. He said, "Diddard? What's that? What was your mama smoking when she named you that?" I told him, "That's my nickname." I didn't get a chance to tell him my real name, because he began to walk towards me. The closer he got to me, I could smell his cologne. It smelled so good that I could taste it. He extended his hand, shook my hand and said, " Taylor here. It's nice to meet you." He was so different. He looked and acted like a boy. He made me want to stay out of my grandmother's closet, because he let me see that there were gay men not wearing women's clothing. As he walked towards the kitchen, it dawned on me, "*That's the guy that I saw with Red behind the shed.*"

CHAPTER NINE

This morning, I was awakened to my mom blasting Toni Braxton's "Seven Whole Days". I get up to see why she is so happy. When I walk into her bedroom, she's standing in her mirror dancing and singing the lyrics loudly. That's when I noticed that she's got a new haircut, and her hair is just like Toni's now. It's a nice cut and fits her quite well. When she realized that I was standing in the doorway, she turned and looked at me with a very stern look. Then she said, "Don't leave this house today! Do you understand?" I replied with, "Yes." When I turned around, my sister was standing there smiling with her backpack. She hugged me and whispered in my ear, "I found your Jane Fonda's workout tape under my bed. You can watch it now, because he's not here today." Wow! I was amazed that my little sister even knew that my stepdad didn't like me watching the video. A few minutes later, my little brother came running up with his backpack, he grabbed my leg, and started yelling, "Diddard!" He is the only one that seems to want me around. Everyone else is trying to figure me out, so we don't really talk much. My sister is hardly ever here, because she is normally with her dad or her best friend. She always found a way to get out of being at the house. After prying my little brother off my leg, my sister said, "Come on! I think I hear the bus coming." They quickly walked out the door to catch the bus.

Once they were gone, it was just my mom and me. She continued dancing and singing in the mirror. Then, Peebles' song came on, and she really started spinning and singing. In the middle of one of the spins, she said, "Don't be making any long distance calls on my phone today either." Ironically as she said that, the phone began to ring. My mom answered, and it was Aunt Doll. Apparently, she has come down from Chicago to help my granny and Aunt Fanny run the restaurant. We will see how long that lasts, because both my great-aunt Doll and my granny are bossy, and they both generally want to run everything. My mom hangs up, and she lets me know that my great-aunt Doll wants to see me that evening. I was so excited to see her and her husband, Uncle Vern. My mom grabbed her keys and purse, and she began to head out the door. I looked out the window to make sure that she was gone, because I was ready to watch Jane shake her booty. While looking out the window, I noticed that my mom was just sitting in the car with a very upset expression on her face. She opened the door and walked back towards the house. When she made it to the door, she snatched it open and screamed, "The damn battery is dead! Someone left the lights on all night!"

My mom grabbed the phone and called the restaurant to let my granny know she was going to be late, but my granny didn't answer the phone. My great uncle Duke answered and told her, "Your Aunt Fanny isn't feeling well. You need to get your ass here now!" She slammed the phone down, and she began to call my stepdad's job. His boss answered and said, "He hasn't shown up yet, because of truck trouble." My mom replied, "Truck trouble? He hasn't got there yet? He left here three hours ago! I haven't heard anything from him!" I could see and feel the pain/rage growing in her! It was hard seeing my mom upset, so I decided to walk to my sister's room and watch Jane. I put the tape in the VCR, and I shook my hips until I got tired. I didn't care who saw it now. After 30 minutes or so, I was tired. I decided to take a quick nap on my sister's bed.

A few hours later, I heard a very familiar song playing. It was the "*Young and Restless*" theme song. I quickly jumped up and joined my mom in the living room to watch it. We might have been 10 minutes into the show when the phone started ringing. Normally, my mom is upset when someone interrupts her soaps, but she didn't seem to mind this time, because she was trying to figure out what was going on with her husband. She answered the phone and it was him. He began to explain to her what happened. He said, "Baby, the truck stopped on me, and I didn't have any change to get a payphone. I finally got it to work, and I just made it here to work." She yelled, "That doesn't make any sense! I am not boo boo the fool!" They continued to argue for a few more minutes before she hung up the phone. She walked back into the living room, looked at me, and she asked me, "Who are all these guys that you have been around? How old are they?" I replied with, " Most of them are between 16 to 20. Then, there are few that are older, but they are just like mentors and father figures." My mom said, "Ummm huh!" Then she asked, "Has anyone been messing with you? Has anyone in the family touched you? Talk to me son." As soon as I was about to rip the band off and start talking and tell her how my stepdad's nephews had been messing with me, the front door opened. We both were surprised. Then, we began to hear my granny sing, "This is my story…." My granny always sang that part of "Blessed Assurance" whenever she walked into a room or called someone on the phone. When she walked into the room, she stopped singing and looked at us and said, "Well hello my darlings!" It was so comforting to see my granny. Her presence always cheered the room. She told my mom, "Girl, I need you and your cousin, Sharone, at work. Dee is the only cook there, and Duke's ass walking around with his lips poked out. I am taking Fanny to the doctor, and Doll is spending some quality time with mama." Then she looked at me and said, "Diddard, you are going to go with your great-aunt Doll to take your great-granny to run some errands. She needs help getting around the city." I got so excited! Then the phone began to ring again. My mom answered the phone, and it was Him again… my step-dad. Her voice began to change because she was getting upset. My step-dad told her that his nephew, Cornbread, needed to come stay with them for awhile, because he kept getting into trouble. They argued for a few minutes before she finally hung up the phone. Then, her and my granny walked into her bedroom. I couldn't believe my ears! He was coming to stay here? I suddenly began to feel my stomach sink as I began to think about my past childhood experiences with him and his brother. Both of his nephews had been in and out of jail, and they were around 18 or 19. Every time that I was alone with them, they both would take turns trying to stick their penises in me. It wouldn't normally work because they both had big ones. However, one memory stuck out like a sore thumb. One night, I spent the night at their house. The next morning, I was awakened by his brother trying to force himself inside of me. This time, he was able to get inside of me, because I screamed once it entered me. That scream woke up Cornbread. He jumped up and knocked his brother off me, but he only did it to try to get inside of me himself. He continued to try to get inside of me until the bedroom door opened. It was their little sister. She just looked at us with a shocked look on her face, and she closed the door. I thought she was going to get help, but she never told anyone what happened. I was awakened from my trance when my granny walked back out the room, and she looked at me and said, "Diddard, pack a bag, because you are coming to stay with me for a while to help your great Aunt Doll and your great granny." I was too excited to hear that, but my mom wasn't. She looked at her mom and asked her, "Why are you always taking him away from me?" As I packed my bag, my granny walked to her car, and my mom followed her fussing about her taking me. I made sure that I grabbed Jane Fonda and the new socks and bloomers that my great-granny had bought me. I couldn't find my shoes though. My little brother must have been playing with them, and they might have ended up in my mom's room. While I am searching the house for my shoes, I see a pair of my step-dad's bloomers in the corner. I couldn't resist to urge to check to see if his bloomers were full of streaks like the gay guys that are taking all of this medicine. When I looked at them, I was amazed because he had a small streak too. I began to think to myself, "Well maybe it isn't a gay thing. Men are probably just full of shit!"

CHAPTER TEN

That thirty minute drive seemed like eternity. My granny focused her attention on driving, my mom kept looking out the passenger window, and I continued to think about my step dad's streak in his bloomers. My granny finally broke the silence when she said, "I forgot to tell you that D'Rae is graduating from Spelman in May. We have to figure out how to get down there for her graduation." A few short minutes later, we pulled into the parking lot of the family's restaurant. Once inside, my granny began greeting the customers, my mama began working, and my cousin, Sharone walked up to me and gave me a big hug. My uncle Duke was sitting in the corner eating a corn beef hash sandwich like he thought he was invisible. My granny asked me, "Do you want something to eat Diddard?" I told her, "No, I am not hungry right now." I decided to walk outside and take a thrill. I was excited to see what or who I would see on my walk. There were many different eateries and department stores on the strip. As I was walking through the parking lot, an older Caucasian woman spoke to me. She said, "Hello there! You're such a hunk!" Then out of nowhere, I heard my great Aunt Doll yell out, "He sure is!" It startled me, because I wasn't expecting her to be outside, but she had stepped outside to smoke a cigarette. I smiled and thanked her for her compliment, and I continued on my walk. A few steps later, I noticed a uhaul parked in front of one of the stores. I began to get curious, and I felt something in my gut that made me wonder if it was some gay guys again. My curiosity got the best of me, so I decided to get a closer look. I walked across the parking lot to the store that was closest to the uhaul. When I was walking to the door, two unfamiliar gay guys walked out with their hands full of bags. One of them looked at the other and said, "Bitch, come on! Let's go!" As they were pulling off, the clerk opened the door and yelled back inside asking, "Did it go through?" Then, she closed the door behind her while shaking her head. As I started walking back through the parking lot, I heard Uncle Vern's voice. He was telling me to come get in the car. Aunt Doll's window was down. She said, "Amey told me that you would be near Stein Mart." Amey is what my Aunt Doll called my granny, while the rest of the sisters called her Ames. When I got in the car, I realized that my great granny was also in the back seat. Then, I remembered that I was supposed to be showing them around while they took my great-granny on her errands. I didn't really know where we were going until I began to hear them discuss that we were heading to Pine Bluff. Great-Granny had made some ceramics for her cousin that was in the hospital. Thirty five minutes later, we pulled into the parking lot of the hospital. We walked into the hospital, and my Aunt Doll is leading the way. I guess someone must have told her the room number, because she walked right to the elevator, pushed the button for the 4th floor, we got off the elevator, and we walked right to the room of my great-granny's cousin. Aunt Doll pushes the door open, and I see a small older lady that I hadn't seen before. She was laying in bed watching *Judge Judy*. The room was cold and lonely. My great-granny sat beside her, and she began talking to her cousin. Aunt Doll sat beside her mom, and Uncle Vern and I stood on the wall, because there were only two chairs. After thirty minutes of standing, I decided to take a walk around the hospital. After I had walked to the entire hall, I decided to take the stairs to see what else I could see. After taking the stairs, I opened the door to the fifth floor. As soon as I began walking down the hall, I began to hear some familiar voices. Someone said, "What? Bitch naw!" When I made the complete corner, I noticed that I saw some familiar faces. I didn't know any of their names, but one of them knew my name. He said, "What brought you to the Bluff? I see you're making your rounds all across the state now." Then, I felt a heavy hand touch my shoulder. It was Big Dane. He asked, "What are you doing here?" I told him, "I am here with my family." Big Dane then informed me that they were there checking on Ray Ray. That sounded familiar to me, because I remembered hearing someone say that he was sick before, and he was dying from the disease that had gotten really bad. Two other guys started walking out of the room arguing with each other. When I looked closely, I realized that it was the two guys that I had seen at Stein Mart earlier. Now, the uhaul in the parking lot of the hospital made sense. They were dressed very nicely. I guess they changed their clothes after they left the store. They got so loud until the security guard said, "Either y'all bring the noise level down, or everyone is going to have to leave!" One of them didn't take his warning seriously, because he began to cuss at the security guard, snap his fingers, and roll his neck. Big Dane grabbed my hand and said, "Come on! They are doing too much." He led me into the hospital room. There were three other guys sitting in there, and Ray Ray. They were all just laughing and having a good time. I could tell that they were trying to make him laugh, because they were saying some corny jokes. When I looked at him, he didn't look like the rest of the guys that I had been seeing. He was very boyish looking, light skinned, pretty skin, pretty teeth, and a very nice smile. He did need a haircut, but that didn't take away from his beauty. Every now and then, his body would begin to shiver like he was cold. In between the shivering, he was able to finally ask me, "What's your name?" Then, he looked at Big Dane and asked, "Is this my new gay daddy?" Everyone started laughing! Big Dane told him, "Chile no! If anything, he is your new gay brother." The guy in the corner started laughing so hard that he hit the guy on the left. Once everyone had gotten a good laugh out, Ray Ray looked at me and said, "You are fresh meat. I wish I wasn't in this bed, but I can't get around with all this stuff they got in me." I asked myself, "*What kind of disease causes you to not be able to move like that? I thought he had AIDS. I didn't know that would cause you not to be able to move.*" When he stopped talking, everyone else began to introduce themselves. The cute dark skinned, very dapper guy spoke. He said, "Hey grandchild! I guess I am your granny, Brandi. This is your Aunt Nickie." Everyone started getting ready to go, but Ray Ray asked Big Dane, "Will you please stay behind to talk to my nurse? My uncle never came to talk to her like he promised." Once everyone started walking out the room, I sat in the chair beside his bed. His energy was so cool and comforting until he began to shiver again. He looked over at me again and said, "You're such a young tender! I have chills laying here, but I don't have anyone to bring me something to put on other than this gown. I began to feel tired and weak." Ray Ray began to look away from us like he was daydreaming, and he began to be really quiet. While Ray Ray was preoccupied, Big Dane began to educate me about gay families. Big Dane said, "Gay families are people who build brotherhoods, friendships, and a bond when you don't feel accepted at home." I found that to be an interesting explanation. I asked him, "Why do I hear people calling each other brothers, but I see them messing around with each other?" He said, "They are just fast in the pants. They don't have shit else to do. All the girls around here are snacking." That didn't really help me, because it made me realize that I didn't want to be in a gay family, if they are supposed to be brothers but they are having sex with each other. Right as we were finishing our conversation, the nurse walked in the room. She was so beautiful. She looked at me with a smile. Then she said, "Oh my God! You're Denise's son! I worked with your mom at Church's Chicken back in the 80's. You're all grown now, and you're handsome!" Big Dane walked out the room to go to the restroom. She asked me, "How do you know them? They are a bit older than you." Ray Ray began to shiver. That's when I asked her, "Will he be okay with the disease he has?" She asked, "What?? What disease? He doesn't have a disease! He is here for something else." I was so confused! They are saying that this man is sick with something else! The nurse told me, "He will be okay for now. He doesn't have any family other than his sister in Dallas, and his mean uncle that lives here. Both of his parents are deceased." Ray Ray slowly came out of his trance and said, "Yeah, they are putting me out of here soon, because I don't have health insurance." The nurse moved his cover back to adjust him in his bed. He started shivering more and said, "I wish my uncle would at least bring me some socks and underwear to keep me warm. That's the least he could do with the money my mom left me, but because I am gay, he says that I don't need it." That made me remember the socks and bloomers that my great-granny had just bought me which I had packed for my stay at my granny's. The more he talked about how his gay family had kept him company, but he still needed the essentials like underwear and socks made me sad for him. I started getting emotional, and I felt my eyes beginning to water. I decided that I had to get out of there before the waterworks began. I immediately jumped up and said, "I have to go check on my folks." As I was about to open the door, Ray Ray said, "Please don't leave without saying goodbye. I like your vibe." As I started walking down the stairs, I began to feel really bad for him. I was so grateful to still have my family, but I could tell that I was disappointing them. As soon as I entered the fourth floor, I saw Uncle Vern walking the hall. He asked me, "Where have you been? Don't get lost." I told him, "I won't get lost. I saw a young friend here in a room." He quickly asked, "Young? What friend? Why is he here?" I snapped and said, "I had heard a rumor that he had a disease but I learned that it wasn't true." As I said the words to him, I couldn't help but remember all the rumors that I had heard about me that weren't true either. Then, I asked him, "May I see the car keys? I need to get some things out of my bag that my buddy needs." As I walk to the car, I see Cuna, Tee Tee, and Aunt RiRi's mom. Tee Tee said, "Hey Terrell! Did you see the baby?" I didn't even know she was here. I'm here with my great-granny. They all gave me a hug. Then they said, "Come check on us on the second floor before you leave." I smiled, agreed to see them later, and I continued to walk to the car. When I made it to the car, I took out my socks and bloomers that were still wrapped in the package that my great-granny had them in when she bought them. I guess it was a blessing that she bought me these. To think, I was ungrateful when she offered to buy them. Then, I began to wonder, *"If a gay family is supposed to be there for you when your real family isn't, why didn't they bring him what he needed? That would be better than making up rumors about him. I am not sure about this gay family thing, but Big Dane hasn't tried to touch me, so I trust him."* I quickly walked back into the hospital, took the elevator to the fourth floor, and I handed Uncle Vern his keys. He was sitting in the waiting area of the hospital looking bored. I told him, "I will be in room 520." I had quickly thought to stop and see Aunt RiRi, but I couldn't stop thinking about poor Ray Ray laying in the bed shivering because he was cold. I knew that I must take him the socks and bloomers as soon as possible. As I walked back into Ray Ray's room, I was greeted by Granny G, Byron, and some skinny guy named Lee. "Well, Well!", Byron said. I walked past everyone and handed Ray Ray the socks and bloomers. Ray Ray looked at me, and the nurse looked around at everyone. Then she said, "All these guys coming here, and they haven't ever brought him anything!" When I looked back at Ray Ray, his eyes were filled with tears. I looked around the room, and I saw that Big Dane and Lee were also about to cry. The nurse told us, "It's almost time for you guys to leave, so I can wash him up and put on his new socks and underwear." She took the socks and underwear out of the packaging. When Ray Ray saw them, he said, "Chile, white socks too? It is already bad that the underwear is white. I can't look down at white socks all day either. It will bore me silly. When you wear socks, you have to have some kind of pattern to them. It won't be so boring to look at." This made everyone in the room laugh. The nurse looked at me and said, " Your heart is gold just like your mom and your grandmother. That is so sweet of you." After she said that, I began to feel good about what I had done. It must have made Ray Ray feel good too, because he couldn't stop crying. Then there was a knock at the door, and the door began to slowly open. It was Aunt Doll and Uncle Vern. Aunt Doll said, "Diddard, here you go?" The nurse told Aunt Doll what was going on. Once she had brought her up to date, Aunt Doll covered her mouth and said, "My niece in Cleveland has MS too, but it's mild." I gave Ray Ray my number, and I also took the hospital information too. Ray Ray asked me for a hug. As I leaned in to hug him, his hug felt so good until we both began to cry. We held each other for a few minutes while we both cried. I didn't want to let him go. Before I let him go, he whispered in my ear, "You are a true angel. Please don't end up like the rest of these girls."

CHAPTER ELEVEN

A few weeks later, we are preparing for my great-granny's birthday party. My family tended to throw a big birthday celebration for her every five years. I was so excited, because I knew that most, if not all of my great-aunts would be in town. I am still staying with my mom, because my stepdad decided it would be best to listen and honor my mom's request to not allow his nephew to stay with us. After he mentioned it, my mom and him had several heated arguments about it, and when my grandmother added her two cents, he decided to just forget about it. These series of arguments have caused an uneasiness in the house. Whenever I am at home, I just don't feel comfortable, because I always think my stepdad is harboring some anger towards me, because his nephew couldn't come stay with us. This uneasiness only fuels my desire to make long distance calls and run up their phone bill. Whenever I am alone, I pick up the phone, call everyone that's out of town, and I have conversations with them. I mostly call only my great-aunts, because I wanted to get the "regular tea". As I walked to the table to pick up the phone, it began to ring. I looked at the caller ID and it said, "PB Memorial." I answered the phone and before I could say anything, I heard someone, "Hello! May I speak to Diddard?" For some strange reason, I felt a nice warm feeling come over me, and I began to giggle. That's when the voice said, "This is Ray Ray! How are you feeling?" We talked for a few minutes, and he told me, "I was able to wiggle a toe today, and I may be getting out soon. I am going to go stay with my sister and her husband. I am glad that I have somewhere to go, but they aren't very comfortable with my sexuality." I could feel his spirit begin to change as he explained his future living situation, so I decided to tell him about what had been happening on the scene with the other girls. This quickly turned his spirits back around, and he remembered how the nurses had been bringing him different kinds of colorful socks and underwear. I could hear the excitement and joy in his voice as he described his current pair of underwear and socks to me. That made me happy! Listening to him made me wish I had a way to go visit him and watch "*Golden Girls*". Then, I began to hear the door open. I quickly told Ray Ray, " I have to go. I hear someone coming into the house. I will talk with you soon." When I placed the phone on the hook, I turned around and my stepdad walked into the room. He spoke to me, went into the kitchen to fix him a drink, and he walked into the den to begin watching wrestling.

After my stepdad had gotten comfortable, I began to sit and wonder how I could possibly get back to the hospital to see Ray Ray, because I had a little change in my pocket, and I wanted to get some more socks and underwear for him. After a few minutes of thinking, I decided to call Big Dane. When I called him, he happily answered the phone. We chatted for a few minutes. That's when he informed me that they were getting ready to go across the river. I asked him, "Can I go?" Big Dane laughed and said, "Honey, no! You are too young! Plus, you aren't ready for it, and they aren't ready for you! You need to stay from over there!" I quickly told him, "I always go to North Little Rock." He told me, "Baby, across the river is Memphis!" Wow! That makes sense! I had kept wondering why people couldn't go across the river, but they had been talking about Memphis instead of North Little Rock. I explained to Big Dane that I wanted to go see Ray Ray. He told me, "Prince C and Lee are getting ready to go see him in a few. You should call them." Then, I heard Granny Brandi yell out, "Hey Grandchild!" That made me smile. I quickly got off with him, so I could call Prince C before they left the city. When I called Prince C, he answered the phone like it was a business. He answered and said, "Hello! This is the Prince Boutique." I replied, "Hey! This is Terrell!" This caused him to laugh. He asked, "What are you up to?" I told him, "I want to go see Ray Ray." Prince C told me, "That's good, because I have been sitting around most of the day waiting for Lee to go with me. That fool just called me a few minutes ago to tell me that he was riding to Dallas with some guy that he met yesterday."

I told Prince C, "Hold on for a second!" I ran into the den to ask my stepdad if I could go see a friend in the hospital. He quickly said, " I don't care." You could hear it in his voice that he genuinely didn't care. I ran back to the phone, and I told Prince C, "I can go with you. What time should I be ready?" He told me, "Give me 30 minutes or so, I will pick you up." I decided to pack an overnight bag, because I didn't know how this night would end. Forty-five minutes later, he pulled up to the house. I grabbed my bag and dashed out the door. As I walked closer to his car, I could hear the music playing and I could smell his Cool Water cologne. He looked and smiled at me before saying, "Are you ready?" I got in the car and we began our journey. I call it a journey, because this would turn out to be more than just a quick ride to see a friend in the hospital.

A few minutes later, we were hitting a couple of corners. As he would pass by the guys walking on the street, he would blow his car horn at them. The next thing I know, we were riding by the penitentiary. I asked him, "Why are we riding here?" He told me, "This is where trade is." I told him, "That can be dangerous." He quickly let me know, "I like danger." We rode around the penitentiary for a few more minutes before we stopped at the McDonald's. When we went to the drive-thru window, Prince C began to flirt with the young guy at the window. The young guy was smiling and blushing really hard. Prince C flirting landed us two free apple pies. When he was about to drive off, he reached into his pocket, grabbed a card, and handed it to the guy. He smiled and told him, " Give me a call sometimes." Then, he pulled off.

I don't think we made it two blocks before I saw another uhaul. I began to smile, because I was wondering who was driving this one. As we pulled beside it at the traffic light, I tried my hardest to see who was driving. Prince C kept easing up to the truck to see who was driving it. Apparently, he was interested too. When we finally got close enough to see who was driving, it was an older Chinese couple. They both must have noticed that we were trying to see who was in the truck, because they both looked at us, waved, and smiled. We returned the gesture before driving off when the light turned green. Prince C laughed and asked me, "Do you know them?" I told him, "I thought you knew them." We both had a good chuckle about that traffic light moment. Then, we continued to the hospital.

Prince C jumped onto Riceville Highway and began to speed down the highway. His beeper started to beep, and it kept beeping. I noticed that he began to look worried. When Shanice came on the radio, I began to dance and sing along with her to lighten the mood. However, he just ignored my silly antics and continued to focus on the highway. Forty-five minutes later, we pulled into the parking lot of the hospital. By this time, he had probably had about ten alerts from his beeper. When we walked into Ray Ray's room, it was empty. Prince C dropped to his knees and began to cry! I felt some tears forming in my eyes too. Then, we heard a familiar voice that said, "Hey guys!" We turned around and it was one of Ray Ray's regular nurses. When she looked into our faces, she quickly said, "Wait! I can tell that you guys are upset, but he's fine. His sister surprised him and picked him up this afternoon. He is going to live with her in Dallas." Prince C jumped up, grabbed me, and he began to hug me tightly! I had never felt a hug like this before. You could tell that he needed it. My grandmother always hugged me, but none of her hugs have ever felt like this one. Prince C hugged me and cried. The nurse handed us a piece of paper with Ray Ray's aol information on it and said, "This is how you can contact him." *Damn! I need to set up an aol account, so I can talk to him.* We thanked her and walked out the room.

The ride back to Little Rock was really quiet. Prince C seemed really focused and worried. When we got back to Little Rock, he told me, "I need to make a quick stop by my house first." When we walked into his living room, Shay was sitting on the sofa. She was about to stick herself with a needle when Prince C walked back into the room and told her, "Bitch, Juan is on the prowl!" The next thing I know, it looked like we were in an action movie or something, because Shay grabbed her things, jumped up, and she darted out the front door. Prince C continued to pick up things and hid them. I asked him, "May I use the restroom?" He ignored me and continued to hide his belongings. I decided to find the bathroom and use it. When I walked into the bathroom, I saw a bunch of nasty bloomers and socks, and there were alot of medicine bottles on the counter. This really made me begin to stress and get worried. I decided to check my underwear to make sure that they were clean. Before I had a chance to check them, I heard a really loud thump! Then, I heard another one. That's when I heard Prince C yell out, "Leave me alone!" I could hear in his voice that he was scared. I could feel my heart begin to palpitate with each thump that I heard. I didn't know what to do! I was so scared! I quickly found a window in the bathroom, and climbed through it to get away from this madness! Once I was out of the house, I began to run! I ran for blocks! I was running to my grandmother's house. She lived like 20 blocks away.

By the time I make it to my granny's house, I see a lot of out of town license plates parked at my great-grandmother's house and my great-aunt Fanny's house. My family was beginning to arrive for my great-grandmother's celebration. I decided to stop by my great-grandmother's house. The closer I got to the side door, I heard a very smooth sounding voice coming from the house. I couldn't tell who was singing, but it sounded really nice and calming. When I walked into the house, I realized that it was my great-uncle, Minister Doug, who was singing. He was singing to my great-grandmother, my Aunt Fanny, Aunt Doll, Aunt Bubbles, Aunt Dot, and Uncle Bubba. They were all sitting there listening attentively, swaying, and rocking to the beat of the song. My great-uncle, Minister Doug, was singing his version of Lou Rauls song, "You Will Never Find Another Love Like mine." When he finished singing, everyone started clapping. Then, they all began to hug me. When I made it to my great-aunt Bubbles, she said, "What have you been doing with yourself? Please don't become a suckling of the tit too." I had to laugh at what she said, because I knew she was talking about my grandmother's children. Out of all of my grandmother's siblings, she was the only one that was still taking care of her grown children. Then Aunt Fanny said, "Alright now!" That was her way of stopping my other aunt from talking. Aunt Doll looked at me and asked, "What's wrong?

Come with me." She leads me into the front bedroom. As we are walking towards the room, we pass by some more family members. It was Uncle Vern, Uncle Duke, Uncle Jimmy (Aunt Dot's husband), and Aunt Bubble's son, Senior. They were sitting in the living room watching the game. We finally make it to the bedroom and sit on the bed. As I began to pour my heart out to Aunt Doll, my great-granny came into the room, and she sat down to listen to it too. I started to explain to them everything! I told them about the medicine bottles, check writing, uhauls, and the dirty bloomers which seem to be caused by the medicine bottles. Before I could tell her anymore, Aunt Doll cut me off and said, "Oh my God! Poor thing! This is too much for you, and you are way too young for this experience." Aunt Doll grabbed me and pulled me into her as she began to embrace me. My great-granny grabbed my face, pulled it up to her, and said, "As long as you have on clean bloomers, be it colorful or not, and you have on clean socks, that's all you need to be worried about right now son."

CHAPTER TWELVE

It's morning, and I am awakened by the smell of salmon patties cooking. I rolled over and laid there for a few minutes enjoying the aroma. While enjoying the scent of breakfast, I couldn't help but think about Prince C and Ray Ray. I was wondering if Prince C was okay, and I was hoping that the guy didn't hurt him. Then, I couldn't help but wonder how Ray Ray settled in Dallas. As I continued to think those different thoughts, I could hear the television in the living room. The news lady said, "Happy New Year's Eve!" I couldn't believe that the year was almost gone, and the holiday season had gone so quickly. I really enjoyed spending time with my family this season. I spent a lot of time with my great aunt Doll and Uncle Vern. I am not sure why they are leaving so soon, but I overheard that my grandmother had told her, "Take your ass back to Chicago." After a few more minutes of me thinking and pondering, I decided to finally get out of bed to see if there were any salmon patties left. When I walked into the kitchen, I noticed that they were all gone. My Uncle D had only made enough for him. I couldn't believe that he didn't make enough for me or his sons. I decided to just go get on the computer and chat with Ray Ray. Right before the dial up started, the phone began to ring. When I checked the caller ID, I noticed that it said, "Cleveland, Ohio." I quickly picked up the phone and answered. I said, "Hello!" It was my great-aunts, TC, Janice, and Phoenix. I was so glad to hear their voices, because none of them came home for the holidays this year. My aunts were so busy chatting amongst themselves that it took them a minute to realize that I had answered the phone. While they were chatting, I could hear them talking about why my Aunt Doll was leaving so quickly. I didn't want to hear them talking about that, so I told them, "Granny isn't here." They all quickly replied with, "Okay." Then out of nowhere, Aunt Phoenix said, "And stay out of my sister's closet!" This made all three of them begin to laugh uncontrollably. Aunt TC stopped the laughter with her questions. She asked, "Were you in my closet when you were staying with me too?" I told her, "No, I wasn't." I quickly ended the conversation by saying, "I have to go! I will talk with you all later. Goodbye!" I had to end the call as fast as possible, because they were beginning to make me angry. I didn't like when they teased me about the closet incident, and apparently it was the new running joke of the family. I will be so glad when it is old.

After that conversation, I decided to try to call Prince C to check on him. Before I had a chance to pick the phone back up, it began to ring again. This time, it was Byron. He said, "Hey Diddard!" That made me laugh, because I knew he was only calling me that to tease me about my nickname. After I answered back, he told me, "We are hanging today. Big Dane is on his way to pick you up." I was so happy that they thought about me. I had begun to spend most of my free time with Granny Brandi, Big Dane, Byron, and this guy named Lee who was literally beginning to annoy the hell out of me. We ended the phone call, and I began to get dressed as quickly as possible. When I was dressed and waiting on Big Dane, I decided to give Prince C a call, but he didn't answer the phone. That really began to make me worry even more. I called Big Dane's house, and his roommate told me that he had already left to pick me up. I decided to go outside and sit on the stoop.

Ten minutes later, Big Dane pulled up to pick me up. When I opened the car door, it was him and Devon. Big Dane made a few stops before finally making it to his place. When we made it back to his house, I was surprised to see how many people were already there. There were probably 15 or more people in the house. As I was walking by two guys, I overheard them saying that they were all going out that night in Memphis. There were drag queens practicing their lip sync numbers for the night, two guys appeared to be sitting in a corner getting high with a needle, some were putting on make-up, eyelashes, and wigs, and a group of guys were smoking weed. This all continued for a few hours, and I just sat there and watched the show.

Three hours later, three new guys walked into the house. They all made them a drink and sat down to watch the guys perform. It didn't take long before I noticed that one guy kept watching me. He was about 5'10", brown skinned, pretty brown eyes, and he had this swag that was alluring to me. After about five minutes of us smiling and looking at each other, he got up and came and sat beside me. He said, "What's up? I am Kevin. What's your name?" I replied, "I am Terrell." We tried to continue our conversation, but the more we tried to talk to each other, this guy kept interrupting our conversation. He was definitely trying to cock block. Kevin finally got sick of him and whispered in my ear, "Let's go sit in my car and talk." I smiled and followed him out to his green Neon with dark tinted windows. Once we got inside his car, he began to butter me up really good. He was saying all kinds of stuff like, "You know you're beautiful right?" I had never been called beautiful by such a gorgeously handsome man. The more and more that I looked into his brown eyes, I began to be mesmerized and slowly fell into a trance. I began to feel my member grow with each word that he said to me. My trance was broken by the hard knock on the window. When I looked up, it was Granny G and Granny Brandi. Granny G was standing there with her right hand on her hip, and Granny Brandi had on a full face of make-up, one eyelash, and no wig. They both were quite upset. After Kevin rolled his window down, Granny G said, "What are you doing to him? He is way too young for you! He is just a baby! Terrell, get your ass out of that car!" They continued to raise hell with Kevin! Out of nowhere, we began to hear a car horn blowing. The blowing got closer and closer. Then, it finally pulled up. It was Shay and Chris. Shay began to yell out her window, "Bitch! Bitch, trade has killed Prince C!" Shay kept saying it over and over again while crying. I couldn't believe my ears! I just sat in Kevin's car, and I could feel tears begin to fall down my face. Shay said, "Everyone is meeting at Byron's house now!" The next thing I know, every-one was jumping in their cars and leaving. They were moving so fast that they all forgot about me. They left me sitting there in Kevin's car. Kevin's friends jumped into the backseat, and he pulled off. The next thing I know, we are pulling up to an unfamiliar townhouse that was downtown. It was a very nice townhouse, but I quickly noticed that there weren't any cars there. Everyone began to get out except me. I didn't know this house. Kevin came back to the car and opened my door. Then he said, "Come on in! Everything is good!" Those damn brown eyes got me again, because I just smiled and jumped out the car.

Once inside, I noticed that there was a guy sitting at the round dining room table. The guy was really skinny. He had on a tied up blouse, he had finger waves with a ponytail, and his legs were crossed. Kevin asked him, "Have you heard about your brother Prince C being killed?" The guy answered him with a grunt of acknowledgement, but he kept his eyes fixed on me the entire time. It was like he didn't even blink. No matter what Kevin asked him, he would answer it but watch me at the same time. I guess he was trying to figure me out. The skinny guy told Kevin, "I talked to your daddy today. He's still in Detroit. He wouldn't be happy with what you brought home." Kevin ignored him. Then he told Kevin, "Oh! I forgot you don't even live here." The skinny guy's eyes stayed locked on me. While Kevin and the other two walked through the town-house, I sat there nervous and scared. I could hear Kevin and some guy arguing in the back. Then, they walked outside while still arguing with each other. When the door closed behind them, the skinny guy jumped up from his seat and he started walking towards the stereo. In mid stride, he asked me, "What's your name?" I told him, "I am Terrell." He replied back with, "Hey Terrell! I am Pumpkin." He turned on the stereo, and he began to lip sync to, "Three is a Crowd" by Milira. While he performed his song, I kept asking myself, "Where have I heard Pumpkin before?" I knew I had heard the name before, but I couldn't remember. As I sat there trying to remember where I had heard that name before, I couldn't help but wonder if Kevin had forgotten about me. Even with the music playing, I could still hear Kevin and the guy outside. They were still arguing.

Finally, Kevin came back inside. He walked up to me, grabbed my hand, and he began to lead me upstairs. We walked into this really nicely decorated bedroom. He motioned for me to sit on the bed. After having me sit down, he began to take his clothes off. Once he was naked, he started taking my clothes off. He pushed down on the bed and he began to grind on me. Before he could get a good motion, the news came on, and they were talking about Prince C's murder. Kevin rolled off me, and he began to cry. Then, he put his clothes on and walked out the room. After he was gone for a few minutes, I decided to put my clothes back on. He was gone for hours, so I just sat there waiting on him. After so long, I decided to lay down and go to sleep. The next morning, I rolled over to a stranger. It was a high yellow, bald head, tall and medium build man sitting on the edge of the bed. He looked at me and said, "Who the

118

fuck are you, and why are you in my bed?" I told him, "I am Terrell." With a mean look still stamped on his face he said, "I am Daddy West."

CPSIA information can be obtained
at www.ICGtesting.com
Printed in the USA
LVHW081810071022
730138LV00014B/511